NEW

NEW

PAMELA MALA SINHA

PLAYWRIGHTS CANADA PRESS
TORONTO

Jacket design by Jacob Whibley and provided courtesy of Necessary Angel Theatre
Company
Author photo © Sara Krulwich

Playwrights Canada Press
202-269 Richmond St. w., Toronto, ON M5V 1X1
416.703.0013 | info@playwrightscanada.com | www.playwrightscanada.com

For professional or amateur production rights, please contact:
Rena Zimmerman, Great North Artist Management
350 Dupont St., Toronto, ON M5R 1V9
416 925 2051

LIBRARY AND ARCHIVES CANADA CATALOGUING IN PUBLICATION
Title: New / Pamela Mala Sinha.
Names: Sinha, Pamela, author.
Description: A play.
Identifiers: Canadiana (print) 20230540570 | Canadiana (ebook) 20230540627
  | ISBN 9780369104670 (softcover) | ISBN 9780369104694 (EPUB)
  | ISBN 9780369104687 (PDF)
Classification: LCC PS8637.I633 N49 2023 | DDC C812/.6—dc23

Playwrights Canada Press staff work across Turtle Island, on Treaty 7, Treaty
13, and Treaty 20 territories, which are the current and ancestral homes of the
Anishinaabe Nations (Ojibwe / Chippewa, Odawa, Potawatomi, Algonquin,
Saulteaux, Nipissing, and Mississauga / Michi Saagiig), the Blackfoot Confederacy
(Kainai, Piikani, and Siksika), néhiyaw, Sioux, Stoney Nakoda, Tsuut'ina, Wendat,
and members of the Haudenosaunee Confederacy (Mohawk, Oneida, Onondaga,
Cayuga, Seneca, and Tuscarora), as well as Metis and Inuit peoples. It always was
and always will be Indigenous land.

We acknowledge the financial support of the Canada Council for the Arts, the
Ontario Arts Council (OAC), Ontario Creates, the Government of Ontario, and
the Government of Canada for our publishing activities.

For Rubena

Storyteller, Dancer, and Teacher

The World was all before them, where to choose
Their place of rest, and Providence their guide:
They, hand in hand, with wandering steps and slow,
Through Eden took their solitary way.
—John Milton, *Paradise Lost*

Let me not pray to be sheltered from dangers,
But to be fearless in facing them.

Let me not beg for the stilling of my pain,
But for the heart to conquer it.
—Rabindranath Tagore, Nobel Laureate

PLAYWRIGHT'S NOTES

My parents immigrated to Canada in the 1960s: my mother was a dancer in Uday Shankar's troupe, and my father was recruited from the London School of Economics by the Universities of Hawaii and Manitoba, and McGill. He chose Manitoba because he was excited about the snow! They built a family from a small group of bachelors and married couples: Hindu, Muslim, Sikh, Christian—it didn't matter—they celebrated everything together. My cousins are my cousins not by blood but through the love that came of those lifelong friendships.

If I am honest, the desire to write this play came from a place of rage and sadness. When I hear of an Indian or Chinese-born person being yelled at—"Go back to your own country!"—I want to scream back: this is their country. They came of age here, gave all they had, and we are all beneficiaries of those gifts of knowledge and love. *They were young here once.* But how would people know this when there's a gap in the cultural narrative? How would they ever know the Indian- or Chinese-born elder they yelled at helped change that small college into the respected university their children now attend? Or helped design the hospital where they were born?

My uncle Biswas was one of those bachelors who became my parents' first "family" here. He called my mother *Bodhi*, sister-in-law, and my father, *Dada*, elder brother. When he died, it felt like I lost Daddy all over again. As I looked through my aunt's old albums of them in their early days in Winnipeg, I saw photos of vibrant, cigarette-holding, Scotch-drinking couples in filmy chiffon saris and skinny ties that looked way cooler than the depictions of "brown" immigrants that inundate present popular culture. So, with a commission from Soulpepper Theatre, I interviewed those aunties and uncles about marriage and loneliness and home. Though the specifics were different, they were a generation like our own, negotiating sex and love and personal identities the best they could while helping to shape the political and social ideals of their adoptive country thousands of miles from the country in which they were born.

Though *New* is a work of fiction, I have tried to capture some of the things they told me in those interviews that mattered to them: the complex nature of love and sacrifice, joyful togetherness and piercing loneliness, and what it means to be thought of as "new"—because of how you look—in a country where you are not new, a country that is your home. With thanks to them, instead of rage and sadness, I offer you the story of *New* with my love, and my gratitude. To my parents Rubena and Snehesh, and Sumita and Shib, Kalpana and Prabir, Hem and Maya, Louella and Ranen, Shashi and Gyan, Asha and Ramesh, Uma and Vedanand and finally Maitreyi: you are my childhood. If anything here offends, I know you'll forgive me. If there is something here you find remotely beautiful, you are the reason.

New was first produced by the Royal Manitoba Theatre Centre in association with Necessary Angel Theatre Company at the Tom Hendry Warehouse, Winnipeg, from November 3 to 19, 2022, with the following cast and creative team:

Qasim: Omar Alex Khan
Abby / Emcee: Alicia Johnston
Sachin: Fuad Ahmed
Sita: Pamela Mala Sinha
Ash: Shelly Antony
Aisha: Dalal Badr
Nuzha: Mirabella Sundar Singh

Director: Alan Dilworth
Set Designer: Lorenzo Savoini
Costume Designer: Michelle Bohn
Lighting Designer: Hugh Conacher
Sound Designer: John Gzowski
Intimacy Director: Sharon Bajer
Fight Director: Darren Martens
Cultural Consultant: Rubena Sinha
Apprentice Director: Jodi Kristjanson
Stage Manager: Michael Duggan
Apprentice Stage Manager: Tori Popp

New was subsequently produced in Toronto by Necessary Angel Theatre Company in association with the Canadian Stage Company and the Royal Manitoba Theatre Centre at the Berkeley Street Theatre from April 25 to May 14, 2023, with the following cast and creative team:

Qasim: Ali Kazmi
Abby / Emcee: Alicia Johnston
Sachin: Fuad Ahmed
Sita: Pamela Mala Sinha
Ash: Shelly Antony
Aisha: Dalal Badr
Nuzha: Mirabella Sundar Singh

Director: Alan Dilworth
Set Designer: Lorenzo Savoini
Costume Designer: Michelle Bohn
Lighting Designer: Hugh Conacher
Sound Designer: John Gzowski
Intimacy Director: Sharon Bajer
Fight Director: Darren Martens
Cultural Consultant: Rubena Sinha
Stage Manager: Sandy Plunkett
Apprentice Stage Manager: Flavia Martin

PRODUCTION NOTES

1970, Winnipeg, Canada. All characters, with the exception of Abby, are Bengali-speaking and of Indian origin.

All Indian characters speak WITHOUT an accent because they are speaking their *own* language, unless indicated "in English" and/or in **BOLD** text. In English they speak with an Anglo Indian accent.

The set in the original production was a one-bedroom apartment divided into a kitchen, living room, and bedroom. Each room represented the kitchen, living room, or bedroom of more than one family and the scenes moved fluidly between the rooms. Location titles were projected above the set, and the front of the stage sometimes represented an exterior location such as the river or the airport.

CAST OF CHARACTERS

Qasim: forties, medical doctor
Abby: forties (not Indian), a nurse, Qasim's lover
Sachin: mid-to-late thirties, professor
Sita: married to Sachin, thirties, dancer
Ash: mid-thirties, ph.d. student
Aisha: married to Ash, thirties, MA student
Nuzha: married to Qasim, early twenties, new bride
Emcee (doubles with Abby)

ACT ONE
SCENE ONE

QASIM's place. Evening.

QASIM—in boxers, smoking profusely—is on the couch, phone in hand, its coil stretched from the kitchen. A near-empty bottle of whisky, a shot glass, and ashtray are on the table before him.

He is a disaster.

QASIM: *(very loud)* I'm here.

Beat.

Ma? I'M HERE, I SAID.

He pours out a shot.

Whatever dowry she wants—what does she want? *Well ask her.*

He throws back the shot.

Of course she can decide later.

Beat.

No—*you* tell him.

Beat.

(*panicking*) *I don't want to talk to the mullah, Ma—* Oh! *Salaam*—yes, this is Qasim.

(*to the mullah*) Yes I agree that Nuzha can decide her own dowry . . .

    He lights up a cigarette—

(*loud, frustrated*) I just said I agreed. Why do I have to—

    Surrendering, he repeats after the mullah while smoking—

"The payment of the dowry will be determined by the bride . . . presented to her by me . . . when she arrives in Canada as—as a demonstration of my commitment."

    He goes to pour out another shot but sees the bottle is empty.

Can I speak to my cousin Salim for one minute?

    Beat.

The tall ugly one.

    Phone in hand, he goes to the bar in search of a new bottle—

Hey, man, can we get this done?! Ma's making me crazy . . . hello—Salim?!

(*yells at them*) *Stop passing the phone around, you guys!*

(*to the mullah*) Oh, sorry—yes, *Mullah-ji*, I have it here.

    He goes back to the coffee table and picks up the aerogram letter, shaking cigarette ash off it.

(*reading*) "I accept marrying your . . . " sorry? Yes, *Mullah-ji*, of course, her first.

As the contract is made on the other end of the line, QASIM
unscrews the cap from a bottle of vodka he's found and takes
a swig.

(mid-gulp) Now?

He reads the contract:

"I accept marrying your daughter, Nuzha Sakila, giving her name to
myself in accordance with the Islamic *Shari'ah*, and in the presence
of the witnesses here with the dowry agreed upon. And Allah—"

He looks at the bottle in his hand . . . then puts it down.

"And Allah is our best witness. *Qubool hai. Qubool hai. Qubool hai.*"

He returns to the couch, letter in hand, depleted.

Beat.

I'm signing it right now.

He casts the letter on the coffee table, not signing.

Beat.

Is Ma there? Can you please put her on.

Beat.

Hi, Ma . . .

(angry) NOW why are you crying?!

Beat.

Why is she crying, Salim?

(*to Ma through the phone*) Well if she's so happy, tell her to eat something, for god's sake! I'm not getting off until 1 know she's eating . . .

> *Beat.*

Good. What?!

> *He stands, in total panic.*

No! SALIM, 1 DON'T WANT TO TALK TO HER. *I DON'T WANT—*

> *He is frozen through the following, barely able to speak.*

Salaam alaikum . . . I'm fine.

> *Beat.*

And you?

> *Beat.*

Yes—1 have it.

> *He reluctantly picks up a photo from the table.*

> *Beat.*

It's . . . *you're* . . . very nice.

> *Pause.*

(*lying badly*) Nice to hear your voice too.

> QASIM *sighs.*

No. No snow yet.

Pause.

You should go back to your party . . . Can you . . . give the phone to my cousin?

He suddenly comes alive again:

I'm going to kill you, Salim—stop laughing like a goddamn hyena! And remember—*her* side is paying for the travel visa, okay? Not ours. Make sure Ma doesn't pay, okay?!

ABBY lets herself in, a sweater over her nurse's uniform, takeout in hand.

(*voice lowered*) I have to go. Salim . . . I have to go. I *will*. Yes—I'll mail it. ·

ABBY heads to the kitchen.

Fine, I'll do it tomorrow—I'm hanging up now!

Salim hangs up. Phone in hand, QASIM remains there, stunned. ABBY continues to unpack the food.

ABBY: (*from the kitchen*) You're different when you're speaking Bengali.

Beat.

QASIM: I sound different?

ABBY: No, you. *You're* different.

Beat. She smiles.

Like there's a whole part of you I've never met.

Still in a state of shock, he doesn't respond.

Say something to me in Bengali.

Beat.

QASIM: *(pained, unable to face her)* "Let me not pray for the stilling of my pain, but for the heart to conquer it."

ABBY: I have no idea what you just said but I loved every minute of it.

QASIM: It's a poem. By Tagore.

Beat.

Let me not *hope* for my pain to stop. Rather, for my heart . . . to overcome.

ABBY: That's beautiful.

Beat.

QASIM: Doesn't come close to the original.

Beat.

He heads to the kitchen and hangs up the phone.

Did you remember to call your father?

ABBY: *Yes.* He hit the roof: "Women are meant to be nurses, Abigail Marie!"

ABBY shrugs.

Maybe he's right. He is a doctor.

QASIM focuses on ABBY.

QASIM: So am I. And I know you're going to be a great doctor.

ABBY: *If* I get in.

QASIM: *When* you get in.

Beat.

QASIM turns to the food.

ABBY: You think I can do anything, don't you?

QASIM: When you put your mind to it, you CAN do anything.

ABBY's arms encircle his waist.

ABBY: That's how I got you.

She rests her head against his back, not letting go.

SCENE TWO

Three months later.

SACHIN and SITA's bedroom. Morning.

SACHIN, in a three-piece suit, carries in a cup of tea for SITA.

SACHIN: Sita. I have your tea . . .

He places it on her bedside table. Awakening, she sits up.

SITA: I was dreaming about Leela.

SACHIN straps on his watch in silence.

Pocketing his wallet and keys, he passes a cardboard box near the bed.

SACHIN: Anything in there you like?

SITA: Tell them we don't want their garbage clothes.

SACHIN: They came from my boss's wife.

SACHIN searches the bedroom.

Have you seen my coat? It's getting chilly.

Sitting up, SITA gestures to an ugly tweed coat in the box.

SITA: Wear that one. It's only missing ALL the buttons.

SACHIN smirks. SITA pulls the covers to her chin.

SACHIN: You will come to the faculty party . . .

SITA: Is that a question or a demand?

SACHIN: They need to see we're united in our ambitions, Sita—

SITA: We're not. We're here because of yours.

He finds his coat and exits the bedroom.

Why didn't you tell me a letter came yesterday?

SACHIN: Because it was from my brother.

SITA: He wants more money.

SACHIN: My cousin is getting married.

SITA: More money so HE can look like a big shot at a wedding!

SACHIN: This is why I didn't tell you.

SITA: We don't have any more this month! He should be able to stand on his own two feet—

SACHIN: And WE should be back home looking after my parents and sister, not *him*—

SITA: Let's go back then.

SACHIN: You'd be sweating in my mother's kitchen if we were there.

SITA laughs.

SITA: Don't pretend you're saving me from that.

He watches her a moment.

SACHIN: I'm late.

He comes back and kisses her on the forehead, then heads for the door.

SITA: Why won't you ever say her name?

Her question hangs between them, demanding an answer.

SACHIN: I'll be home at six.

Hearing the door close behind him, SITA buries herself deep into the bed again as lights come up on ASH and AISHA's kitchen.

AISHA dumps out the contents of her book bag on the kitchen table, where ASH is rolling a joint.

ASH: Hey—watch the weed!

*Finding her address book, she heads to the phone and starts
to dial.*

It's barely eight—who are you calling?

AISHA: *(into the phone)* Oh. Hi. Yes, this is Aisha—Chopra—would
it be possible to see Dr. Lehman today?

ASH: *(stops mid-roll)* Doctor?

AISHA: No, it's not an emergency . . . Monday? Yes, great, I'll take
it! Thanks, bye.

She hangs up. ASH is already staring at her. She's beaming.

I'm late.

Beat.

My period. It's late.

ASH rises to hug her.

Beat.

Are you happy?

ASH: Are you mad? Of course I am.

*But AISHA pulls back to look at his face when a sharp knock
interrupts them. SACHIN enters.*

SACHIN: Qasim riding with us?

AISHA: (*laughs, covering*) Why do you always knock first? You just walk in anyway—

ASH: He didn't call. He must be at Abby's.

AISHA starts repacking her bag.

AISHA: How come he never brings her over here?

ASH: Because he's ashamed of you.

She swats him with a book. He smiles. A secret between them.

SACHIN: I have to teach in thirty minutes.

AISHA: (*to ASH*) Should we get dinner out tonight?

SACHIN goes.

ASH: You go ahead. I want to get a swim in.

AISHA: You're swimming *tonight*?

SACHIN: (*off-stage*) Starting the car!

ASH: Let's go out *after* your appointment Monday. I'll take you to your favourite place.

AISHA: (*confused*) What's my favourite place?

ASH: (*with a quick, close grab*) **Expensive!**

She pushes him off, pretend-mad. He runs out after SACHIN.

About to lock up, she remembers her keys. Grabbing them, she exits the apartment as lights come up on the hallway.

AISHA locks her door just as ABBY emerges from QASIM's place next door, a coat over her nurse's uniform.

AISHA: *(in English)* **Oh. Hi.**

ABBY smiles, shy.

ABBY: Hi.

AISHA notices ABBY lock up with a key on her own key ring.

AISHA: Things are pretty serious with you guys, huh?

ABBY: You could say that.

AISHA: You should hang out with us some time.

ABBY: I'd . . . *love* to—

AISHA: What about Sunday? It's a big day for Qasim.

ABBY: *(surprised)* It is?

AISHA: It's a *puja*—sorry—*ceremony*—for him and Sita. A Hindu thing.

ABBY: But Qasim's *Muslim*—

AISHA: Doesn't matter—it's because they're close. The ceremony just makes that bond official.

ABBY: I'd love to come! I'm always telling him I want to know more about his . . . world.

Beat.

Sorry—that must sound so ignorant.

AISHA: Not at all. And if it's any consolation, we're always telling him the same thing. He should have brought you over long before now.

ABBY smiles.

Beat.

ABBY: Will the ceremony be in Bengali?

AISHA: Yes. But Sachin will make sure you understand what's going on.

ABBY: Thank you.

Beat.

I want to know which customs are meaningful to him—which aren't. I think it's important for me to know these things when we're . . . planning a future.

AISHA: Then we shall start this Sunday, at 8 p.m.!

(on the move) Oh, not here—at Sita and Sachin's. 217, just—

ABBY: Under you.

As AISHA rushes away, ABBY—happy—watches her go.

SCENE THREE

QASIM's place. Evening.

*QASIM lies on the couch, arm over his eyes. ABBY emerges from
the bathroom, heading for the bedroom.*

ABBY: Can we sleep at my place tonight? I really need a change of
clothes.

*She throws a couple of things into a small overnight bag on
the bed.*

Love? Can we go?

She goes to the bedroom door. He hasn't moved.

QASIM: I love you.

ABBY: I love you too.

QASIM reaches his hand up to her. She comes over to take it.

Beat.

QASIM: Do you believe me?

ABBY: What is going *on* with you?

She comes around the couch, not letting go of his hand.

(*studying him*) You're up to something.

Beat.

Are you . . . HIDING something in there?!

Suddenly she jumps astride him, playful.

QASIM: **Abby, stop—!**

ABBY: *(digging in his pants pocket)* Something you might put into a small, *velvet—*

QASIM cuts her off with a kiss.

Pause.

I think my landlords are going to sell.

QASIM: **How do you know?**

ABBY: Every time they say hello to me lately, they say it in a really sad way—like something bad's coming.

(imitates them, exaggerating) "Hello, Abby . . . "

He can't help but laugh. She removes a lock of hair from in front of his eyes.

Maybe I should move in with you. I'm here most nights anyway.

QASIM doesn't respond.

(embarrassed) We don't have to talk about it now.

QASIM: **Abby, there's something . . .**

ABBY: Oh, I'm coming Sunday night!

QASIM: **Coming where?**

ABBY: Your ceremony . . . Aisha invited me. Why didn't you tell me it was such a special / night—

QASIM: *(blurts)* **I'm married.**

ABBY: What?

QASIM: I'm . . . *married.*

>   *Beat.*

ABBY: Are you joking?

QASIM: **No.**

ABBY: What do you mean you're—

QASIM: I'm sorry—

ABBY: You've been married all this time?

QASIM: **Not all this time!**

ABBY: *Not—?*   QASIM: **Three months—***not all this time.* **Three months.**

QASIM: **She blackmailed me!**

ABBY: WHO DID—

QASIM: **My mother! She wouldn't eat unless I agreed.**

>   *Beat.*

>   *ABBY stands, unsteady.*

(soft, careful) **She's *eighty*, Abby.**

>   *Beat.*

She wouldn't even take water!

Pause.

ABBY: I have to . . .

But she doesn't know where to go.

QASIM: I don't know how . . . it was like—it was happening to someone else.

Beat.

Like I wasn't even there.

Beat.

(*breaking*) And then . . . like it never happened.

Pause.

ABBY: You lied.

QASIM: I didn't—

ABBY: You lied to *me*.

They stare at each other.

Why didn't you tell me?

QASIM: Telling you . . . would have made it real.

Beat.

ABBY: Why are you telling me now?

Beat.

Why now, Qasim?

QASIM: She arrives tomorrow.

In one motion she heads for the bedroom to grab her bag. Frantic, she searches for her purse. He sees it first and goes for it in an attempt to stop her from leaving, but she rips it out of his hands.

I love you, Abby.

She turns on him.

ABBY: Do *NOT* say that to me!

She goes. QASIM, stunned, stares ahead.

SCENE FOUR

Airport arrivals gate. Saturday, September 19, 1970.

QASIM, a bag on the ground next to him, holds roses and a sign. SACHIN stands near but not close.

PA ANNOUNCEMENT: Your attention, please. British Airways regrets to announce Flight 1010 arriving from Glasgow is delayed. We repeat, British Airways Flight 1010, arriving from Glasgow, is delayed.

They stare straight ahead.

SACHIN: The only reason I know you're married is because you needed a goddamn ride!

QASIM: I'm going to be sick.

He shoves the flowers and sign at SACHIN *and rushes off. With no other option,* SACHIN *holds up the sign, revealing the name "Nuzha Khan."*

NUZHA, *exhausted and dishevelled, appears, barely able to push her luggage cart loaded with suitcases. Seeing the sign with her name, she is suddenly shy, and quickly bows her head.*

NUZHA: *Salaam alaikum.*

SACHIN *takes a tentative step towards her. Her eyes remain downcast through the following:*

(in English) **I want change . . . but my this** *(her cart)* **too big . . .**

SACHIN: These are for you.

He offers her the bouquet and the sign. She politely takes them.

Beat.

SACHIN *then takes the sign back.*

Sorry, you don't need that   *you* know who you are!

He laughs at his bad joke.

Beat.

Not knowing what else to say:

How was your flight?

NUZHA: It was day, then night, then day again.

SACHIN: Yes.

Beat.

It's very . . .

NUZHA: Far.

Beat.

Do you—we—live far from here?

SACHIN: Half an hour, maybe. But everything here is half an hour from where you're going.

NUZHA: Really?

SACHIN: I mean you have to drive.

SACHIN: Unless you live on campus.

NUZHA: You don't look like your photo.

SACHIN: Sorry?

NUZHA: You look different. From your photo.

SACHIN: I look . . . ?

Beat.

Oh god, I'm Sachin—Qasim's friend! I *drove* him here—

NUZHA: (*embarrassed, she looks at him*) Oh, I thought . . . I'm so sorry!

SACHIN: No, no, it's my fault—actually, it's Qasim's fault! He made me hold this *FUCKING* sign—

NUZHA: That's why you didn't dress up.

Beat.

SACHIN: The flowers are from him.

SACHIN is mortified—for her and for himself.

About to collapse from exhaustion and stress, NUZHA finds a place to sit. SACHIN picks up QASIM's bag and places it on the cart.

Beat.

NUZHA: Is he . . . coming back?

SACHIN: Of course! He just needed some air.

SACHIN takes a step away, scouring the area for any sign of QASIM.

Beat.

NUZHA: (*not meeting his eyes*) Are you married?

SACHIN: Yes.

Beat.

NUZHA: Do you have children?

Beat.

SACHIN: Not yet.

Beat.

Do you want children?

NUZHA: I have to meet my husband first.

> *SACHIN laughs, then spots QASIM with a bouquet of tulips. Seeing NUZHA in the flesh, he stops short, at a loss for words.*
>
> *NUZHA stands, her eyes lowered to QASIM through the following:*

QASIM: *Salaam alaikum.*

NUZHA: *Wa alaikum salaam.*

SACHIN: (*to QASIM*) **Where the hell were you?!**

QASIM: **I wanted to get something else in case she didn't like roses.**

NUZHA: **I like . . . roje.**

> *She looks up at him briefly, then down again.*
>
> *Beat.*

QASIM: You look tired.

> *NUZHA adjusts her sari.*

NUZHA: I'm sorry, I didn't have time to—

QASIM: (*quickly*) I only meant you must be feeling very tired after—

NUZHA: You look like your photo.

QASIM: Yes.

NUZHA: That doesn't always happen.

Beat.

My cousin met a man in New York that looked like her photo's grandfather.

QASIM: That's terrible!

NUZHA: (*defensive*) They're in love now.

QASIM: That's . . . good?

QASIM *looks at* SACHIN *for help.*

SACHIN: (*to* NUZHA) Everyone is looking forward to meeting you. We're doing *Bhai Phota* tomorrow night. We'd love you to come.

NUZHA: (*excited*) They have Brother's Day in America?!

SACHIN: No! Sita—*my wife*—has been wanting to do this for some time. With your . . . husband.

QASIM: (*to* NUZHA) Sita's like my sister.

NUZHA: You don't have a sister.

SACHIN: She's *like* his sister. Not like HIS sister.

Beat.

QASIM: I bought you a coat!

QASIM *presents the bag to* NUZHA. *Taking it, she pulls out the coat and puts it on.* QASIM *doesn't quite know how to help. It's too big.*

(*disappointed*) I can exchange it.

NUZHA: It's very warm—

QASIM: There are some gloves in the . . . if you don't like them
I can—

NUZHA: (*finds them*) I like blue.

QASIM: Good!

SACHIN: Where are her boots?

QASIM: What boots?

SACHIN: (*to NUZHA*) What do you have on your feet?

> NUZHA *lifts her sari to reveal jewelled flip-flops.*

QASIM: Oh my god!   SACHIN: She can't wear those!

QASIM: (*to SACHIN*) I'm not an idiot!

NUZHA: It's fine.

QASIM: I'm an idiot!

SACHIN: Why don't I bring the car / around—

QASIM: I'll do it.

SACHIN: No, you stay! I'll—

QASIM: JUST GIVE ME THE KEYS, MAN!

> SACHIN *quickly hands* QASIM *the keys and he goes.*

> *Registering* NUZHA's *alarm,* SACHIN *pulls a scarf from the bag.*

SACHIN: Oh, almost forgot. He got you this.

NUZHA wraps it around her head and shoulders in an Indian "shawl" style.

Beat.

NUZHA: Does he . . . have a temper?

SACHIN: No. He's just scared.

NUZHA looks in QASIM's direction, feeling very alone.

SCENE FIVE

ASH and AISHA's place. Later.

ASH rolls a joint in the living room. The door opens and SITA flies in, SACHIN following close behind.

SITA: Tell them how old she is!

ASH: I was wondering how long it would take for you to get here.

SITA: Where's Aisha?!

ASH: Bathroom.

(to SACHIN) How old is she?

SACHIN: Twenty, twenty-two / maybe?

SITA: QASIM IS FORTY-THREE YEARS OLD.

SACHIN: *Okay, Sita—*

SITA: He lied to us.

SACHIN: He didn't *lie.*

ASH: By omission he did.

SACHIN: He said he . . . forgot.

SITA: FORGOT TO TELL US HE GOT *MARRIED*?!

SACHIN: Why are you yelling at us? We didn't marry her—

The phone rings twice, indicating a long-distance call.

ASH: Aisha, trunk call—they got the line!

(*answering*) **Hello? Yes, I'll hold.**

AISHA emerges from the bathroom, her eyes red.

AISHA: Hi, Sita—

ASH: Are you crying?

AISHA shakes her head and grabs the phone.

AISHA: Ma? MA?

(*excited*) YES, I CAN HEAR YOU.

(*faking it, laughing*) DOING VERY WELL.

Beat.

No. Nothing new—NO, JUST COURSE WORK—

Beat.

Nothing new in that department either . . . NO NEWS, I SAID.

Beat.

(*fights tears*) Doctor said very healthy.

Seeing AISHA *unable to keep it together,* ASH *takes over.*

ASH: **Hi . . . No, no! All fine . . . I was getting too jealous to hear your voice!**

Beat.

I'm defending my thesis in January—did I tell you? Yes! Your son-in-law will be a doctor soon!

Beat.

ASH *sighs.*

No, not a *medical* doctor . . .

He checks in with AISHA.

One second—

ASH *hands the phone back to her.*

AISHA: We'll call you next time, okay?

(*louder*) Ma?

(*frustrated, to* ASH) She can't hear me.

(*into the phone*) MA? Yes! A MONTH today! WE WILL CALL—

The line cuts out.

ASH: **Four hours waiting and it still cuts out.**

AISHA forcefully circles the date of the call on the wall calendar with a pencil, the tip breaks.

AISHA: They're only interested in one thing! "When will you have / a baby—"

ASH: Who wants a toke?! I need one after that nightmare.

AISHA: Don't call my parents a nightmare!

SITA: Aisha . . . he doesn't like to see you cry.

ASH: *(to AISHA)* It makes me crazy, baby.

AISHA meets his eyes. They share a moment between them.

SACHIN: *(teasing them, to SITA)* We should let them "make up."

AISHA: What you're imagining is a lot more interesting than what actually happens around here.

ASH: What's that supposed to mean?

SACHIN and SITA laugh.

AISHA: Did you forget our wedding night?

(to SITA) Your Mr. Romantic here stood me up!

ASH: That's a lie!

AISHA: His mother hung a wall of garlands around the bed—you know how they do that . . . well, she tied one rose for every twenty-four jasmine flowers on every string. Not one mistake.

(*looks at* ASH) Ask him how I know that.

SACHIN: (*amused, to* ASH) How does she know?

ASH: (*practised*) She was waiting so long, she had time enough to count them.

SITA: *ASH!!*

AISHA: When he finally walked in, from where I was sitting it looked like he had roses on his shoulders and one in each of his hands.

(*to* ASH) He looked beautiful.

ASH: Can I talk now?

AISHA: Be my guest!

ASH: Samir—my best friend since school days—had flown all the way from Calgary to India *for the weekend* to be at our wedding! I had to see him for more than five minutes!

SITA: But it was your wedding night!

ASH: And Samir's only night! I have the rest of my life with her—

AISHA: And when he finally *did* show up, I couldn't *wait* for him to rip down that stupid wall of flowers—

SITA: (*to ASH*) Tell me you did at least that—

AISHA: He pushed them aside so *gently* . . . not a single flower fell . . . We talked all night. I don't remember falling asleep. When I woke up in the morning he was gone.

   Pause.

ASH: (*defensive*) It was a pretty good honeymoon, if I remember correctly.

SACHIN: That's more than Nuzha will get. Qasim took no time off—

AISHA: Poor Nuzha!

ASH: Why don't we give them a party?

AISHA: We could do it at the International Centre?

SACHIN: The "India" room is too small for a reception.

SITA: The Ukrainians lent their room to us once.

ASH: For the *Christmas* party—and that was because we were hosting last year.

AISHA: What about Germany? Or Japan? They're the perfect size.

ASH: (*to SACHIN*) Why can't we get a bigger room? You're on the board—

SACHIN: We get that room for a *dollar a year* and you're still complaining.

SITA: The India room can fit fifty at least. Fatima can do the dessert, and Vandana and her South Indians can do the vegetarian. I'll make chicken!

SACHIN: Or we could do the party at our place tomorrow. Just us.

SITA: Tomorrow is my Brother's Day *puja*.

SACHIN: Do it another night. Nuzha just got here—

SITA: You can't do something another night that's supposed to happen on a specific *date*—

SACHIN: Why can't you?

    SITA reacts. ASH deflects.

ASH: Did I tell you my wife is a spy?

AISHA: A blueprint from the land registrar's office is hardly top secret.

SACHIN: What's your new point of attack?

AISHA: We prefer the term "civil disobedience."

    Beat.

A theatre. They'll expect us to run out the main doors but—

ASH: Aisha found *options*.

    AISHA doesn't compliment. SITA stands.

SITA: Decide what you want to do tomorrow and let me know.

SACHIN: We'll do what you *planned*, Sita.

SITA goes.

We always do—

SACHIN follows her out.

Once they've gone:

AISHA: Why did you stop me from talking?

ASH: You told the whole damn story! Which you know I hate—

AISHA: No, about *babies*—

ASH: I'm not talking to *Sita* about babies!

AISHA: She can always have another one!

ASH: You don't know that!

AISHA: Do you know how it feels to believe in something—*really believe*—that a woman's value isn't determined by her motherhood and then cave to it? It feels like shit, Ash. It really feels like shit.

Beat.

I don't need to see to see Dr. Lehman. I got my period. I'm not pregnant.

ASH reaches an arm out to her. AISHA goes over but he pulls her down onto his lap.

ASH: Listen. You're hot . . . I'm *really* hot . . . Can't we just enjoy that for a while?

AISHA: Tell my parents that.

ASH: *Aisha . . .*

AISHA: WHEN THEY CALL . . . tell them you're hot and I'm hot and you just want to enjoy that for seven *more* years.

She disappears inside the bedroom, slamming the door behind her, leaving ASH in her wake.

SCENE SIX

SACHIN and SITA's place. Evening. Sunday, September 20, 1970.

In the bedroom doorway, SACHIN watches SITA place a sheet over a duvet laid out on the floor. She gets down on her knees and begins to tuck the sheet under the duvet edges.

SACHIN: We should be throwing a wedding party, not a *puja*.

SITA doesn't respond.

I'm just asking you to be flexible—

SITA: Why won't you let me have this?

Frustrated, SACHIN retreats to the kitchen. SITA continues tucking . . .

Do you know only one person ever asked me what Leela looked like? It was Qasim.

Beat.

I told him. About her lashes . . . butterflies. Her mouth—*your* mouth. He knows the face I see when I cook, when I dream, when I wait for you to come home . . . the face I never stop seeing.

She touches her heart.

In here he's already my family. But this *puja* will make it real.

SACHIN takes this in, then "helps" by placing a small puja *table on the sheet.*

AISHA enters in upscale hippie fashion, carrying fresh roses.

AISHA: *(drily)* She dressed up.

NUZHA appears, overdressed and dazzling in her "new bride" regalia, covered in gold from head to toe, followed by QASIM and ASH.

SITA: Nuzha! Welcome.

QASIM: I need a drink.

SACHIN leads QASIM to the kitchen.

AISHA: Where do you want the flowers?

SITA hands AISHA a bowl.

SITA: Just the petals.

Seeing NUZHA settling on the sheet:

Oh, that *lehenga* is too beautiful for the floor. Please, take the sofa.

NUZHA perches obediently on the edge of the couch. ASH settles on the sheet with the bowl while AISHA rips the heads off the roses.

(to ASH) Ready?

ASH nods—barely. SACHIN gets a plate of sweets from the kitchen and places it on the puja *table and sits cross-legged in front of it.*

So . . . I've asked Ash to say a few words about tonight's *puja* because not everyone here knows what it means.

AISHA: (*teases SITA, to NUZHA*) By "everyone" she means us *Muslims.*

Through the following, alone in the kitchen, SITA lights a diya *(lamp) and prays over the* puja *tray, which holds a conch, sandalwood, the* diya, *a tiny silver glass, and a bracelet of red thread.*

ASH: (*nervous, standing*) The Bengali ceremony of *Bhai Phota.*

AISHA laughs.

AISHA: Why are you standing—why is he *standing*?!

ASH: For non-Bengali's, *Bhai Phota* is also known as *Raakhi—*

AISHA: (*teasing*) But what's it known as HERE?

ASH: (*irritated*) They don't have it, but I guess "Brother's Day"—

AISHA: I say SISTER'S DAY in CANADA!

ASH: Will you let me finish?

QASIM, drink in hand, stands far off to the side.

Despite the fact that Qasim—as a Muslim—would not traditionally observe this Brother's Day tradition—

SACHIN: (*gestures to QASIM's drink*) Qasim, "as a Muslim," doesn't observe *any* tradition.

AISHA: (*to QASIM*) Why are you standing so far away? / Come closer.

ASH: *Today* . . . these two will make their brother-sister bond official. Before they do that, however, I'd like to ask Sita one question.

SITA enters with the tray, placing it on the puja *table.*

Why the hell didn't you pick me?

SITA laughs.

SITA: Get on with the story, will you!

SITA settles on the floor to one side of SACHIN and rubs the sandalwood to make paste.

Beat.

ASH: (*serious*) Yama and Yami were brother and sister. When Yama died, he became the god of death. And now, because he's stuck in the underworld, they could never meet.

QASIM: Who could never meet?

ASH: Are you deaf? Yama and his sister.

ASH sits.

SITA: And *then*?

ASH: Then nothing. Then, the end!

SITA: That's not the end!

ASH: That's the end!

SITA: But what does it *mean*, Ash?

ASH: (*confused*) What does the story mean, you mean?

AISHA: (*laughing*) You guys are terrible Hindus!

SACHIN: (*to SITA*) Why don't we skip the story?

SITA: (*irritated*) Because I don't WANT to skip the story. I want to / hear—

NUZHA: (*shy, eyes cast down*) Surjo, the sun god, and his wife Sweta had two mortal children: a boy, Yama, and a girl, Yami. When Yama grew up, he became the ruler of the Land of the Dead. Because he had to maintain an account of all deeds and misdeeds in the Land of the Living, he could never leave. He mourned his sister, and she mourned him. Yami wept so much that the gods turned her into the goddess of the night, "Bridging the despair of the sunset with the hope of the sunrise."

Beat.

(*to SITA*) But once a year—on this day—this brother god and sister goddess are allowed to meet . . . renewing the bonds of love between them.

They all stare at her, speechless. NUZHA shrugs it off.

I grew up Muslim in a Hindu neighbourhood. We just paid more attention than you all did.

Despite himself, QASIM smiles. He knows what she means.

SITA: The "bonds of love." Thank you, Nuzha.

AISHA: (*to QASIM, in English*) **Okay, you . . . stop hovering and sit down.**

QASIM sits cross-legged on the floor opposite SITA. With sandalwood on the third finger of her right hand, SITA touches QASIM's forehead and holds it there for the following prayer:

SACHIN: "I put a *phota* on my brother's forehead,"

SITA: "I put a *phota* on my brother's forehead,"

SACHIN: "To make my brother immortal,"

SITA: "To make my brother immortal,"

SACHIN: "Yamuna gives it to Yama,"

SITA: "Yamuna gives it to Yama,"

SACHIN: "As I give it to my brother,"

SITA: "As I give it to my brother,"

SACHIN: "Who may become as tough as iron."

SITA: "Who may become as tough as iron."

AISHA: *(scoffs)* **More sexist bullshit!**

SACHIN: *(to SITA)* Now tie your "bond of love."

    SITA picks up the braid of thread. Tied to it is a tiny bell.

QASIM: You made this for me?

    SACHIN picks up the conch shell and blows into it three times as SITA ties the bracelet around QASIM's wrist. It's a tender moment.

SACHIN: Now bless your new sister!

QASIM: Why? She's older. She should bless me.

SITA: *(horrified)* I am *not* older!

QASIM playfully sticks his head down in front of SITA.

QASIM: You better bless me!

SITA, laughing, pushes QASIM away. He chases her through the following as SACHIN blows the conch continuously:

SITA: *(to NUZHA)* Tell your husband to get away!

NUZHA smiles, enjoying this side of her new husband . . .

Head leading, QASIM chases SITA.

QASIM: BLESS ME, MY DIDI!

SITA: *I am not your DIDI!*

The blowing of the conch masks the knock on the door. It opens, revealing ABBY, shivering in a sparkly dress and too-light coat.

ABBY: Sorry I'm late.

QASIM is stunned. Everyone is stunned.

Beat.

I'm interrupting.

SACHIN: No.

(to ASH) **No, not at all.**

ASH, getting the message, takes ABBY's coat while AISHA brings her over to the opposite end of the sofa from NUZHA.

Let's continue, shall we. Aisha? The flowers please.

AISHA passes the bowl of petals forward.

ASH: (*to NUZHA*) Abby is Qasim's nurse at the clinic.

NUZHA: (*to ABBY*) How long . . . he—you—work?

SACHIN: Take a handful . . .

ABBY: I quit.

QASIM and SITA take this in, then throw a handful of petals over each other. The gesture falls flat.

SACHIN: (*to SITA and QASIM*) Now take some sweets and feed each other.

QASIM stares at ABBY. ABBY stares right back. SITA takes a sweet and shoves it into QASIM's mouth, forcing him to pay attention.

SACHIN stands.

What music you all want to hear? Classical or—

SITA: We're not *finished?*

SITA picks up the silver glass, but SACHIN is already at the stereo. He pulls out an album that is gift-wrapped.

SACHIN: How about this one?

QASIM: For me?

SACHIN: For *both* of you.

Taking it, QASIM hands it to NUZHA to unwrap, avoiding ABBY's gaze. It's L.A. Woman by the Doors.

QASIM: *(delighted, to ASH)* Weren't you just talking about this?

ASH: *(re: SACHIN)* Bastard beat me to it.

SITA approaches SACHIN.

SITA: You didn't finish.

SACHIN: *(kind)* If there's more, I don't remember.

(to QASIM) Why don't you put it on?

QASIM places the record on the turntable as SITA storms off with the puja tray. ASH offers a joint to SACHIN, who waves it away.

ASH: *(to QASIM)* **Crank it, man!**

Through the following, ASH lights up, SACHIN puts away the sheet and duvet, and the men rock out a bit.

NUZHA: *(to ABBY, over the music)* **You . . . children?**

ABBY: I'm not married.

QASIM focuses harder on the liner notes on the album cover.

NUZHA: **Why . . . no marry?!**

ABBY: I'm a nurse.

AISHA: Some women don't want marriage.

NUZHA: *(horrified, to ABBY)* **No marriage?! Why?!**

ABBY digs in her purse for cigarettes. NUZHA takes in ABBY's miniskirt.

You . . . not cold?

ABBY lights up a cigarette.

ABBY: No.

NUZHA: *(re: her own skirt)* **My this . . . too much hot.**

NUZHA giggles.

Your—very good! I *like*—

NUZHA touches the hem of ABBY's dress. ABBY leaps up—

ABBY: Can I get some wine?!

AISHA: We have some upstairs—

AISHA throws ASH her key.

ABBY: *(to ASH)* I'll just have what you're having.

ASH heads to the bar cart.

NUZHA: Did you all decide to live here together?

AISHA: God no! Ash met Sachin at the university a little over a year ago. They were supposed to move into a two-bedroom on campus because of the baby / but then—

ASH: *(quickly)* And here we are! Hindus outnumbering Muslims, of course. Just like back home.

QASIM: *(drily)* You're lucky we left, Hindu boy.

NUZHA: *(confused)* We didn't *leave*. We were forced out.

QASIM: It was a joke.

NUZHA blushes, embarrassed.

QASIM notices his bracelet has come undone.

Sita! It's come open.

ABBY: I'll do it.

Not wanting to draw attention, QASIM offers ABBY his wrist. She takes her time retying it.

Is there some significance to this bracelet?

ASH: **This thread connects Qasim to Sita. Like a birth cord. He is now her brother for life.**

ABBY holds on to QASIM's wrist.

ABBY: It's so lovely . . . and this little bell!

Seeing NUZHA's eyes on them, QASIM pulls his hand from ABBY's grasp. This lands hard, as lights come up on SITA's kitchen.

AISHA watches SITA take a seemingly endless parade of casserole dishes covered in tinfoil from the oven.

AISHA: Are you guys fighting?

SITA: We're not *fighting*—

AISHA: *(over her)* Because if it's over this gong show of a marriage, we just had the same fight upstairs! How do you make someone your girlfriend for a whole YEAR then throw her away the second your wife shows up?!

SITA: Nuzha will hear you!

AISHA: And *THEN* disrespect your wife by not telling her that the love of your life is sitting just two feet away from her!

ABBY: Can l help?

ABBY stands in the kitchen doorway. SITA, covering, gestures to the water jug on the table.

You want me to pour?

SITA nods and continues to bring food out of the oven.

You're a dancer, Sita—right?

AISHA: A *great* dancer! Her teacher is very famous in India. Uday Shankar. Sita danced all over Asia in his troupe.

ABBY: Any relation to Ravi Shankar?

AISHA: His elder brother.

ABBY: You're kidding!

Beat.

l love Indian dance. It's so *intricate* . . . What you do with your hands . . . Can you show me some?

Hesitating only a moment, SITA shows ABBY the gesture for water: as if flowing from the jug in ABBY's hand.

Water.

SITA changes the gesture slightly.

River!

SITA's hands spin gracefully into the petals of a lotus . . . SACHIN, unseen by SITA, stands transfixed in the doorway.

SACHIN: I wish you would do that more.

SITA blushes. Taking a glass of water, SACHIN leaves.

Beat.

ABBY tries the blooming lotus gesture . . .

ABBY: I should probably stick to nursing.

SITA takes ABBY's hands and forms her fingers into a simple flower. ABBY notices SITA's ring.

That's a stunning ring.

AISHA: Sita's teacher gave it to—

SITA stops AISHA.

SITA: I want to . . .

AISHA: (*to ABBY*) You should be flattered. She *never* speaks English.

SITA: (*to ABBY*) Guru . . . me. To *me.*

Sliding the ring off, SITA places it on ABBY's finger.

Sita, you . . . *far, far . . .* but—

SITA taps the ring, then places her hand over her heart.

ABBY: I'm with you.

SITA nods, happy to be understood.

ABBY looks across the room at QASIM who, catching her glance, steps out onto the balcony.

In the background ASH and SACHIN are making their way from the living room to the kitchen to get dinner. SITA serves.

QASIM searches for his cigarettes, then his lighter. ABBY steps up behind him. She hands him his lighter.

You didn't have to pull your hand away from me like that.

They stand in silence for a while.

Finally, he lights up.

Sita's lovely. You never told me she was so sweet.

QASIM: She's not *sweet*—**she's a fireball. You don't know Sita.**

ABBY: Who's fault is that?

She takes the cigarette from his mouth and takes a drag.

Pause.

Nuzha's beautiful.

ABBY: And young.　　　　　　**QASIM: Stop.**

ABBY: What are you two going to talk about?

QASIM: Abby, just stop.

ABBY: *(baiting him)* Why?! They can't *hear* us!

QASIM: (*trying to be quiet*) **Because there's no reason for this!**

ABBY: (*not caring if she's quiet*) Really, Qasim?!

Beat.

You met my *parents*. At forty-two years old, their only daughter finally brought someone home to meet them.

Beat.

Do you remember what they said?

Beat.

QASIM: **Thank god he's not a Catholic.**

Pause.

ABBY: We were so nervous . . . and now you're part of the family. I won't pretend it never happened! I'm not like you—

QASIM: **I'm not denying it / happened!**

ABBY: Then tell her the truth, for god's sake! Go in there right now and tell her you love me and we're happy and we have / plans—

QASIM: **Stop, Abby—**

ABBY: Stop *what*?! Stop fighting for us?! Stop loving you—?!

QASIM: *Stop . . .*

(*pained, tender*) **. . . humiliating yourself. Please.**

ABBY *is stunned.*

She heads for the door.

ASH: (*seeing ABBY*) **Aren't you guys going to eat something?**

But ABBY's fast, moving past NUZHA and AISHA on the couch with their plates. ABBY opens the door, then stops.

ABBY: (*to an astonished SITA*) Thank you for being so nice.

Beat.

I'm not crazy. I'm not a crazy person. I just thought . . . I don't know what I thought.

Beat.

I don't understand. I mean I do—I *do* . . . understand.

(*fights tears*) I just thought I could make it . . .

She runs out.

Beat.

AISHA: (*to QASIM*) Someone should go after her.

QASIM: (*a plea to SACHIN*) **You can.**

SACHIN grabs his coat to follow ABBY out. SITA stares at QASIM. NUZHA, a little curious, goes back to her food.

SCENE SEVEN

Outside.

SACHIN catches up to ABBY, who doesn't slow down—

ABBY: Is it because I'm white!?

SACHIN: Of course not!

ABBY: You can't just throw people away like that!

SACHIN: I KNOW—

ABBY: Then why did you *let him*?!

SACHIN: You think we *knew* about this?! Abby, I only found out because he needed a ride to the airport!

This is all too much for ABBY, who sobs in an avalanche of grief. A car honks, forcing them to move.

ABBY: He doesn't care about me.

SACHIN: Then why did he send me out here?

Beat.

You're shaking.

SACHIN takes his scarf and wraps it around her bare neck.

I can't go back unless I can tell him I've put you safely into a cab.

Beat.

Will you let me do that?

Beat.

ABBY: No.

SACHIN watches her walk towards the main road, alone.

SCENE EIGHT

QASIM's place. Later the same night.

NUZHA stands in the bedroom doorway, peeking across the living room at the closed bathroom door.

When she hears the faucet turn off, she leaps on the bed, twirls once, then jumps and sits—fanning her skirt around her. She pulls down her veil, clearly instructed not to meet his eyes.

QASIM enters and stops short—he has no idea what to do next.

QASIM: Do you want some water? I can bring you some water?

Pause.

You can have mine.

He places the glass on her bedside table and then . . . leaves. NUZHA waits on the bed, unsure. QASIM lies down on the couch.

Pause.

NUZHA: Are you . . . coming back?

QASIM: I thought I'd sleep out here.

Beat.

NUZHA: You don't have to.

QASIM sighs and reluctantly returns to the bedroom. He goes to his side and sits carefully on the edge of the bed, his back to her.

QASIM: You must be tired.

NUZHA: A little.

Pause.

QASIM: One day for every hour.

She doesn't respond. He turns to look at her.

It can take up to a day for each time zone crossed. For your body to adjust to local time.

NUZHA: Oh.

Beat.

I like your friends. They're very nice.

QASIM: (*willing a response*) They . . . liked you too.

NUZHA: You think so?! I hope so.

Beat.

QASIM: Can I . . . shut the light?

NUZHA: (*nervous*) Yes.

The room goes dark, the only light from the lamp in the parking lot outside, drawing NUZHA'*s attention.*

When will the snow come?

QASIM: November, usually. By December it will be waist high.

Beat.

NUZHA: Has anyone ever drowned in the snow?

QASIM: I've never heard of it.

Lifting her skirt aside, QASIM *lies down, his back still to her.*

Nuzha.

Beat.

NUZHA *gulps.*

NUZHA: Yes?

QASIM: You should get some rest.

Not knowing what else to do, NUZHA *lies back stiffly over her fanned-out skirt.*

She stares up at the ceiling . . . filled with a mixture of confusion and relief.

SCENE NINE

The riverbank. Same time later.

SITA stands alone, lit by her flashlight. SACHIN arrives.

SACHIN: Qasim finally left.

Beat.

I think he was buying time so that Nuzha would be asleep by the time he got home.

SITA doesn't respond.

Even if Abby was invited, why would she put herself through that?

Again, no response.

To see for herself, I suppose.

SACHIN pulls his coat tighter.

Nuzha's lovely? It's good you'll have some company during the day when we're all—

SITA: She ruined my *puja*!

SACHIN: How did Nuzha—?

SITA: It was supposed to be a ceremony for Qasim and me, and you turned it into a *party for her when I specifically asked you not to*—

SACHIN: We finished the *puja*!

SITA: You were rushing! You didn't finish *properly*—

SACHIN: They don't even do it "properly" back home—they just follow the priest—you know that. Nobody *cares*, Sita—

SITA: NO—*you* don't care! It was just another stupid ritual that means nothing to YOU, so how could it possibly mean anything to anyone else.

This is loaded and he knows it. He starts to walk away.

That's why you let them burn her.

SACHIN turns on her.

SACHIN: I refused to let some scripture that neither of has ever even *read* tell us what do with OUR BABY—

SITA: So just throw her ashes into a river.

SACHIN: A HOLY river!

SITA: It wasn't *right*—

SACHIN: Letting her rot in the ground was *right*?!

SITA: I WANTED A PLACE TO BE WITH HER—I HAVE NO PLACE I CAN GO TO BE WITH HER NOW.

She turns back to the river. He can't leave like this.

When we let her go, her ashes didn't go straight down—did you see? She was so small . . . there were hardly any. They didn't fall straight down—they were twirling . . . like she was dancing.

Beat.

You left me there.

SACHIN: You said you wanted to be alone.

SITA: I stayed in the boat after you left. The river was so . . . peaceful. The fog looked like smoke floating on water in the middle where we left her and suddenly I felt . . . good. I felt *good*. I wanted to see you then—

SACHIN: You did?

SITA: I stood up. The boat was tippy—I grabbed the edge to steady myself, and when I looked down I saw garbage. Banana leaves, string, flowers . . . rotten petals in shallow water.

Things you throw away. Not things you love. Not things that are a part of you. I thought, one day you'll be under the feet of another sad, sick mother stepping out of another boat. She'll hear the laugh of a child and think, "Is that you, my baby?" But it's not. Just another mother's child slipping on a banana leaf chasing her purple kite along the shore. You will be under their feet in this wet, dirty water and no one will know.

 Pause.

SACHIN: What will be enough for you to forgive me, Sita? What can I do that will finally be enough?

SITA: It doesn't matter what you do anymore. Everything I want . . . everything that matters to me . . . you make me lose.

 SITA goes back inside. SACHIN is devastated.

SCENE TEN

Pantages Theatre. Sunday, September 27, 1970.

A male has-been celebrity in his fifties introduces contestants at a beauty pageant. He carries a mic.

EMCEE: Miss British Colum . . . *yum-yum-bia* . . . Miss Saskatchewan . . . *I'll take that-a-wan!* Miss Alberta, *find me in Room 22, thirty-four-ahhh!*

(jokes into the mic) Now, folks, I don't want you to think I'm a dirty old man because I don't give women a second thought . . . my first thought covers everything!

The audience roars with laughter.

And there you have it, ladies and gentlemen, the gorgeous gams vying for the national crown that will take them to *Miss World 1970*!!!

The audience cheers. The EMCEE *beams.*

AISHA: *(yells unseen)* **Is this a cattle auction?!**

AISHA's feminist group, planted throughout the audience, respond:

FEMINISTS: *(staggered)* HELL YEAH!

AISHA: Are we at a CATTLE AUCTION?!

EMCEE: What the—???   **FEMINISTS:** *(even louder)* HELL YEAH!!!

AISHA appears in the audience.

AISHA: *(into megaphone)* **Can makeup cover the wounds of oppression?!**

EMCEE: *(incensed, to AISHA)* You stop that, young lady!   FEMINISTS: HELL NO!

Several football rattles suddenly blare in the audience.

AISHA: *(into megaphone)* **Feminism is the radical notion that . . . ?**

The EMCEE stands in shock as AISHA runs down the aisle—

FEMINISTS: WOMEN. ARE. PEOPLE!

EMCEE: *(apoplectic, to AISHA) Don't you come any closer!*

—and throws a flour bomb, exploding on the EMCEE.

The audience reacts in the chaos.

AISHA clambers on stage as the EMCEE runs off.

AISHA: *(centre stage, into megaphone)* **WE WILL *NOT* BE OBJECTIFIED!!!**

ASH steps onto the stage from the wings.

ASH: AISHA! We gotta go!

AISHA: **FREE OUR SISTERS, FREE OURSELVES!**

He runs and grabs her.

ASH: *NOW, I SAID!*

They run off stage, entering again elsewhere, out of breath.

I swear to god, Aisha!

AISHA: (*catching her breath*) Is everyone out?

ASH: Everyone except you of course, hanging around on stage!

AISHA: (*laughing*) Did you see the guards blocking the entrance? They looked so confused!

> *She throws her arms around his neck, excited, happy.*

Thank you for coming back for me!

ASH: I had to make sure you didn't get thrown out of the country.

(*serious*) This was risky, Aisha. No more like this one.

> *AISHA lets go of his neck, looking guilty.*

Oh god.

> *She heads to their building. ASH doesn't follow.*

What is it this time?!

AISHA: The criminal code restricting legal abortion. We're joining the national caravan when they get here—

ASH: *Whose* caravan?!

AISHA: (*excited*) The Women's Caucus! We're going to chain ourselves to chairs in parliament—

ASH: That's a federal building—are you crazy?!

AISHA: There were a hundred thousand illegal abortions this year—in *this* country alone. That's two thousand dead—

ASH: You're a foreign student!

AISHA: Twenty *thousand* of those were hospitalized with post-abortion complications—

ASH: YOU COULD GET *DEPORTED*.

It's a standoff.

AISHA: They use hangers, Ash. Or if they're too scared, they douche with Lysol.

Beat. Beat.

ASH: Go home. I'll see you later.

AISHA: You're not coming up?

ASH: I want to get a swim in.

She gently touches his face. He can't help but give in, cradling his cheek in her hand. She leans in for a kiss.

It's passionate, but too quickly he moves away from it . . . not the first time her passion has been deflected.

I can't flake on him, babe—

AISHA: Flake on who?

ASH: A guy from the pool. We started racing as a joke and just kind of made it a regular thing.

AISHA: Oh.

ASH: Do you want to come? It'll be fun.

AISHA: I've had enough fun for one night.

ASH: You're sure . . . ?

She nods.

Cool, babe. I won't be long.

AISHA watches him go . . . She waves, not sure if he saw.

SCENE ELEVEN

Apartment courtyard. Sunday, October 4, 1970.

SACHIN, in pyjamas and overcoat, smokes. NUZHA, coat over her nightgown, is surprised to see him there. She hesitates, unsure if it's appropriate to stay. He sees her.

SACHIN: What are you . . . are you all right?

NUZHA: I . . . wanted to see what a moon looked like in the morning. We don't get that back home.

Standing at a distance, they look at the moon for a while.

It's like it's hanging between the night and morning.

Beat.

I'm going to take the bus today.

SACHIN: Where?

NUZHA: Winnipeg . . . Art . . . Gallery. Aisha says I can easily do it. One bus there, and the same bus home.

Beat.

Once I've seen everything, I'll pick someplace new. This way I have somewhere to go in the mornings like you all do.

SACHIN: All except Sita.

NUZHA: She never goes out?

SACHIN: Sita is incapable of not being good at something. It's why she won't speak English. Or go out alone. If she can't do something right, she simply won't do it.

NUZHA: She goes to the river alone.

SACHIN: Two hundred metres from our window.

They look at the moon again . . . awkwardly alone with each other.

Beat.

NUZHA: When it was bright like this, my mother used to take me to the roof to look. I'd fall asleep up there.

SACHIN: Us too. Even the mosquitoes couldn't keep us off our roof—

NUZHA: Baba would string nets over our cots. Mummy hated the ropes digging into her back, so it was just me and my cousins talking all night long.

Beat.

You know those small compact mirrors? Shazia—my older cousin—would take her compact and shine it at the rooftops of the neighbourhood boys to get their attention.

SACHIN: Ingenious Shazia.

NUZHA: Until the boys got a compact of their own and started flashing us back! The neighbours noticed the light show one night and told my parents.

SACHIN: The end of rooftop romance?

NUZHA: Most definitely the end.

Beat.

I have never seen a sky so clear or a moon so bright.

SACHIN: It's the cold. It gives us the two gifts of the longest nights and a sky more transparent than we could ever have in the heat.

NUZHA: If the longest nights are a gift.

SACHIN takes this in.

SACHIN: Sita's not speaking to me again.

NUZHA: Why not?

SACHIN: No reason. So many reasons.

Beat.

I promised if she married me there would be no children.

NUZHA: You promised *no* children?

SACHIN: I would have promised her the moon to be my wife. She wanted to go on dancing. I wanted her to be happy. When we found out she was . . . of course she didn't want to keep it. I convinced her it was fate. And then—incredibly—she fell in love. With her pregnancy. With . . . *Leela.*

Beat.

She died being born.

Pause.

You know those cradles—the ones they put on the plane for small babies? The whole way here there was an empty cradle waiting in front of Sita's seat. I forgot to cancel it.

NUZHA: It wasn't intentional—

SACHIN: She wanted to bury her baby. I didn't let her.

NUZHA: But Hindus don't bury their . . .

SACHIN: If a child is stillborn we do. A baby's soul has no attachment to their body—they have no "I." We bury them because they're innocent.

Beat.

Now you know. I'm a very bad Hindu.

NUZHA: Muslims bury their dead because if we didn't there would be no body for Allah to resurrect. But it has nothing to do with Allah—there's no wood in the desert. You can't cremate a body if you have no wood. It's a practical thing.

Lights up on the stairwell.

SACHIN: Saying that makes you a very bad Muslim.

NUZHA: Bad Muslim. Bad Hindu. Guess that means we'll both go to hell.

SACHIN: They say your hell is empty because your Allah is a merciful and compassionate God.

NUZHA: And they say you Hindus don't *have* a hell.

Beat.

SACHIN: We're both safe from it then.

NUZHA: In the afterlife anyway.

They smile, comforted in some small way. NUZHA *climbs the stairs, then stops.*

(*her back to* SACHIN) Sometimes when he's sleeping, I let my back touch his. Like an accident. He always moves away.

SACHIN: (*embarrassed*) He . . . doesn't know what he's doing when he's sleeping.

NUZHA: Even when he's sleeping he wants to get away.

NUZHA *reaches her floor.*

You said "her baby." Sita wanted to bury *her* baby.

SACHIN: Yes.

NUZHA: She was your baby too.

She disappears inside. SACHIN *stares after her.*

End of Act One.

ACT TWO
SCENE ONE

*QASIM and NUZHA's place. Evening. Tuesday, November
24, 1970.*

*SITA, AISHA, and an overdressed NUZHA sit in the kitchen in
awkward silence. On the table sit teacups and a foil-covered
casserole dish.*

NUZHA: (*to SITA*) Thank you for bringing dinner again. He'll eat no
matter how late he comes home.

SITA: Does he come home late every night?

*NUZHA nods. SITA picks up the casserole dish and puts it in
the oven.*

NUZHA: Did you both have a love marriage?

SITA: Yes.   **AISHA:** Ash and I were friends
first. We were inseparable.

NUZHA: Friends first is good.

*AISHA studies NUZHA's unhappy face. Through the following,
SITA gathers their cups and puts them in the sink.*

I already have three letters from home asking if there's a baby yet.

AISHA: There's plenty of time for babies! And you have to be careful—at your age it can happen very fast—

NUZHA: (*blurts, upset*) What happen? There *is* no "happen"!

SITA: What do you mean?

NUZHA: At first I thought, he's tired. Then I thought, he works so hard—maybe that's why. And then a month and I think—*soon*? But now it's two months since I've come and he doesn't even . . . try. I don't have anything left to think.

AISHA looks at SITA.

AISHA: Did you know this?

SITA shakes her head no. This is serious.

NUZHA: Children follow marriage. That's what Mummy said. But I can't do it *alone.*

Beat.

What if he . . .

NUZHA stops, afraid to say it aloud.

SITA: What if he what?

NUZHA: Sends me back.

Pause.

AISHA: I have a book you need to read! Once you learn English better—

NUZHA: (*offended*) I read English!

SITA: (*surprised*) You do?

> AISHA *goes to her bag at the door.*

NUZHA: I only get stuck when I speak. Even if I practise a thousand times in my head what I want to say—because of how I look—they've already decided they won't understand me.

SITA: That's why *I* never speak!

AISHA: (*re: book*) It's about how the pressure women feel to be mothers is really just another way to exclude women from jobs outside the home. This book was written to save women exactly like you!

> AISHA *drops the book on the table in front of* NUZHA—*and* SITA.

> SITA *stands abruptly.*

SITA: I have to cook.

AISHA: (*re: casserole dish*) You don't have any of this at home?

SITA: It's not enough—

AISHA: He can make a sandwich!

SITA: I have to cook for my husband, Aisha.

AISHA: My GOD, SITA, there's more to life than being a *wife*—

SITA: No. We're here because we ARE WIVES. Stop pretending we're the same as you.

> QASIM *opens the door.* SITA *flies past him.*

She needs more closet space!

QASIM takes off his coat and shoes through the following.

QASIM: *(to NUZHA)* You can take all the drawers.

AISHA: Why don't you *help* her?

NUZHA: We can do it tomorrow? After you take me on a tour of the city—

AISHA: *(to QASIM)* **You haven't shown her the city yet?!**

QASIM shrugs. AISHA reacts.

(to NUZHA) If there are words in there you don't understand, underline them and I'll explain them to you later.

With a withering look at QASIM, AISHA's gone.

Pause.

QASIM: Aisha gave you a book?

NUZHA: Yes.

QASIM: A woman's lib book?

NUZHA: I think so.

QASIM pours himself a drink. NUZHA watches from the kitchen.

QASIM: *(catching her eye)* Does my drinking offend you?

NUZHA: If it offended me, I wouldn't have said *yes* to your mother.

Beat.

Sita brought your favourite.

NUZHA plates the food, then rinses her hands in the kitchen sink. QASIM does the same. They sit and eat with their hands.

Through the following, QASIM, though polite, barely looks at her.

QASIM: You . . . don't have to dress like that.

NUZHA: Like what?

QASIM: Dress up. You can just be normal at home.

Beat.

NUZHA: This *is* normal.

Pause.

I got a letter from my grandmother today. She wants to know when I can visit home.

QASIM: Does she think money grows on trees here? I can't afford to send you so soon!

NUZHA: She thinks you're rich.

QASIM: I'm not rich.

NUZHA smiles.

NUZHA: You're a doctor. For her that *makes* you rich.

Pause.

Do you notice anything different?

QASIM: Where?

NUZHA: *(re: the living room)* There.

QASIM: *(barely glances)* You moved the coffee table.

NUZHA: The lamp. It's better for reading there.

QASIM: *(eating)* Looks good.

NUZHA: You don't notice anything, do you?

QASIM reaches over to open the fridge.

QASIM: There's no Hi-C?

NUZHA: I finished it—I'm sorry—I should / have left you some—

QASIM: Why sorry? You live here too.

Beat.

I'll pick more up later. I need cigarettes anyway.

NUZHA: I can go with you.

QASIM: You don't have to.

NUZHA puts her plate in the sink and rinses her hands. She sits down again.

You don't have to sit with me. You can go to bed.

NUZHA: *(quietly)* So you can come when you're sure I'm asleep?

Before he can respond, the phone rings.

QASIM: *(answers)* **Hello . . . ? Oh, David!**

Beat.

No problem at all.

Beat.

No, that's fine . . . I can easily do it. Enjoy your day off.

He hangs up and goes back to his food.

I have to work tomorrow. They need me.

NUZHA: There was no one else?

QASIM: No need to look for anyone else.

He puts his plate in the sink and rinses his hands. Returning to the living room, he pours another drink.

NUZHA gets started on the dishes.

You don't have to do those.

NUZHA: I like it clean in the morning.

QASIM: I can do them. Really, Nuzha, you don't have to do / that—

She crashes a pot into the sink.

NUZHA: When they showed me your picture, you know the first thing I asked your mother? If you liked to read. She said you liked medical journals. I told her studying was different from a love to read. She said she was sorry she couldn't answer my question, but she could tell me one thing. I would never have any reason to be afraid of you.

Beat.

QASIM: Are you afraid?

Beat.

NUZHA: I'm very afraid you don't want me for your wife.

She heads for the bedroom, then stops, her back to him.

If you send me back, not one person will be waiting for me at the airport.

She goes. QASIM *is still, then throws back his drink.*

SCENE TWO

Bus stop. Same night.

QASIM *waits. A bus approaches—its doors open.* ABBY *gets off. They face each other, saying nothing.*

QASIM: I would have paid for a cab. I don't know why you're so stubborn.

ABBY: Where's your wife?

QASIM: In name only.

Beat.

Asleep.

Pause.

ABBY: Why am I here, Qasim?

QASIM: Why aren't you cashing my cheques? It's two months since you quit and you haven't cashed a single one.

He takes an envelope of cash from his pocket and offers it to her. She pushes it away.

ABBY: So you can feel like a hero?!

QASIM: You don't have a job because of me—

He tries to put the envelope into her coat pocket.

ABBY: I SAID NO.

Pause.

I have a job. At the hospital. Part-time but they like me.

QASIM: I suppose that fool Russell had something to do with that.

ABBY: Doctor Carling recommended me—yes. He said I'd be a good fit.

QASIM reacts.

Pause.

QASIM: Your MCAT is coming up.

ABBY: I don't feel much like studying—

QASIM: You have to think about your future!

ABBY: My future is no longer your business. Medical school or otherwise.

Pause.

Tell me something.

QASIM: **Anything.**

ABBY: Did you fuck me the night you got married?

QASIM: (*shocked*) **I never *fucked you*. I would never—**

ABBY: Sex isn't love if you make a fool of the person.

This lands hard. She walks past him, needing space.

How long was this marriage a plan?

QASIM: **IT WASN'T A PLAN!**

She doesn't respond. He tries again.

My mother was visiting Calcutta when she saw her old neighbour from the village! Ma thought she had died in the riots with everyone else. Nuzha is that neighbour's *granddaughter*. Those two old women arranged the match—I had nothing to do with it! NOTHING. When I told my mother I wouldn't go through with the marriage, she refused to eat.

ABBY: (*scoffs*) She would have eaten eventually—

QASIM: *No.* **She wouldn't have. She would have died.**

A bus approaches and stops, but ABBY doesn't get on.

Do you think I'm a good doctor? I have no passion for it. I would have made a better teacher.

ABBY: What does that have to do with anything?

QASIM shakes his head. ABBY starts to walk away—

QASIM: What choice did I have?!

ABBY: One that wasn't your mother's?! One you could have made on that *balcony* / that night—

QASIM: We don't have choices—

ABBY: Who doesn't have choices? Indians? Doctors? You don't have choices because I'm *white*?

QASIM: This has nothing to do with RACE!

She starts to leave again.

(*desperate*) My cousin Salim? He's not even my real cousin—we have no blood family left! Everything burned in the partition— her village, her family . . . *everyone*. I'm all she has.

Beat.

I don't know why it had to be THIS girl . . . but I couldn't let my mother die over it. Not after everything she barely survived.

Beat.

ABBY: No one could ever make me do something I didn't want to do.

QASIM: Because you CAN want, or not want. Partition / took that—

ABBY: (*incredulous*) *Partition* made you do it?!

QASIM: Yes! Everything now is what we OWE *them*.

Pause.

ABBY: I need to go home.

QASIM: Let me drive you.

ABBY: I want to walk—

QASIM: I can't bear to be alone with her.

ABBY takes a long look at him and goes.

SCENE THREE

QASIM's living room. Afternoon. Friday, November 27, 1970.

NUZHA stands alone in the centre of the room. The clock ticks . . .

She walks backwards and leans against the wall, slowly turning to rest her forehead against it. She bangs her head against the wall once. She goes to the stereo and puts on the Doors; it's the same song from the evening of the Brother's Day ceremony.

She starts to move, half-hearted yet awkwardly sensual.

The door opens. SACHIN, dressed for work with briefcase in hand, watches NUZHA, unseen. She stops abruptly, as if suspended. Aware he's witnessing a private moment, SACHIN steps back into the hallway, but NUZHA catches him.

Beat.

NUZHA: I'm not very good.

She turns off the record player.

They spend so much money. Dance lessons, singing lessons—you don't even have to be good at it. You just have to know *how* . . . so they can marry you off.

SACHIN pulls a bus schedule out of his breast pocket.

SACHIN: I brought this. It's a bus schedule. So you don't have to wait outside in the cold wondering when the bus will come.

NUZHA: *(taking it)* Thank you.

She walks over to the couch and lays it flat on the coffee table.

SACHIN: That's not how you read it.

NUZHA: Oh.   **SACHIN:** Do you want me to—?

NUZHA: If you have time?

SACHIN: *(reluctant)* A little time.

Setting down his briefcase, he slips off his shoes but keeps his coat on.

He sits at the opposite end of the couch from NUZHA, the schedule between them. He folds it into three precise parts. When he's done:

You open it here to find the route that you want . . . then pull it wider to look for the times. Mondays to Fridays on this side . . . and Saturdays—look here. But you won't need Saturdays because Qasim can drive you where you want to go.

NUZHA: He works on Saturdays now. He volunteers at the free clinic.

Beat.

SACHIN: Well one of us can drive you. The buses are slower on weekends.

NUZHA: They drive slower on the weekends?!

SACHIN: The *wait* is longer on the weekends.

With a pen from his breast pocket, SACHIN circles a stop.

This stop is home.

Without moving from her spot, NUZHA leans in to look more closely.

NUZHA: *(reads)* **Cory . . .**

SACHIN: **Corydon.**

NUZHA: **Cory-don.**

Beat.

What does this column mean?

SACHIN: Don't look there—it will only confuse you. This is the only column you have to look at when leaving from home. Find the time you want to go *here* . . . then be at the stop out front five minutes before.

NUZHA: It will really come at these times?!

SACHIN nods. NUZHA is amazed. She slides the schedule closer.

But it says the last bus coming back is at 3:22 p.m.? That's so early.

He slides it back to himself.

SACHIN: You see this column? **Carlton and Graham?**

He circles it.

This is the stop you get off at when you go to the **art gallery.** The times coming back are listed here. Up to midnight—

NUZHA: *(impressed)* Midnight!

SACHIN: Now that you know what time the bus will pick you up, you can do other things while you wait.

NUZHA: Other things?

SACHIN: Go to the Bay, have a tea . . . with the time you know you have before the bus arrives.

> *NUZHA nods, excited.*

I should go.

> *He puts his pen into his breast pocket but doesn't stand.*

NUZHA: What bus goes to the university?

SACHIN: There's nothing to see there. Only buildings.

NUZHA: You're there.

(quickly) And Ash. And Aisha.

> *Beat.*

Show me.

> *Beat.*

SACHIN: **This column. University Crescent.**

> *NUZHA gestures for SACHIN's pen—he gives it to her. She circles the stop then puts the pen on the table. They stare at the pen.*

I really should go.

NUZHA: I can make tea?

SACHIN: I have papers to mark.

Taking the pen, he goes to the door.

NUZHA: You don't like me either.

SACHIN: Of course I like you.

Pause.

I don't know how to help you.

Beat.

NUZHA: Hold me?

SACHIN: Nuzha—

NUZHA: I just want someone to . . . *hold* me.

After a moment, he walks back to her and sits. Awkwardly he reaches out his arm and she tucks under it. She takes his other arm and wraps it around her. He co-operates, finally holding her close.

Despite himself, we see him feeling her in his arms. She sighs deeply—he immediately moves away.

SACHIN: Where's my briefcase?

It's at the door. As he steps into his shoes, NUZHA starts to sob. SACHIN is unable to move in any direction.

Nuzha . . . *please.*

She can't stop.

Did you grow up in a joint family?

NUZHA *barely shakes her head no.*

I did. We were twenty in our house. Cousins, aunts, uncles . . . our family stayed at one end, at the opposite was a courtyard, the kitchen, and a well. I woke up thirsty one night. As I was walking to the kitchen I was struck by how quiet it was . . . that's why I heard her. She was standing on the edge of the well, ready to jump. I cried out—she grabbed the pole because I startled her . . . the exact opposite of what she wanted to do. I pulled her down on top of me before she could jump—she fought me so hard . . . but we never made a sound—we didn't want to wake anyone. Finally she collapsed on top of me. I don't know how long I held onto her like that. My little sister.

Beat.

He was my father's best friend. If he stayed for lunch, he would take his afternoon nap at our house. One of those afternoons he found my sister and told her with those buckteeth and flat figure no one would ever want her for a wife. No one would ever think of her as beautiful. He told her because of this, she would never know the love of a man. That's what he called it—*the love of a man.* He raped her as a favour.

Beat.

She was so thin no one knew she was pregnant. My mother arranged the abortion. My brother takes care of her now. I send a little extra to him when I can . . . But it makes Sita angry when I do.

NUZHA: Knowing all this she still gets angry?

SACHIN: She doesn't know.

NUZHA: She wouldn't be angry if you told her the reason.

Pause.

What happened to your sister?

SACHIN: She never married—that man was right about that. But he was wrong about everything else. She knows the love of her brothers. And she is the most beautiful girl in the world to me.

Pause.

NUZHA: Why did you tell me that story?

Pause.

I know why you told it.

NUZHA stands.

Matter-of-factly and without an ounce of seduction, she drops the top fold of her sari, exposing her blouse and midriff.

SACHIN doesn't move.

Slowly, NUZHA walks towards SACHIN until she is standing directly in front of him.

You are *not* that man.

He still doesn't move.

NUZHA's arms encircle his neck—another suspended moment . . .

In one motion he lifts her: her face hiding in his neck, his face buried in her hair he carries her to the bedroom, sari trailing behind.

SCENE FOUR

ASH and AISHA's place. Night. Saturday, December 19, 1970.

On the couch, wrapped in a blanket, ASH watches the end credits of The Mary Tyler Moore Show.

AISHA reads, her head in his lap. She laughs suddenly.

ASH: What?

AISHA: Nothing.

She laughs again.

ASH: *What,* for god's sake?!

AISHA: "Women have very little idea of how much men hate them."

ASH: Who says that?

AISHA: Germaine Greer.

He gets up and flips through the channels.

Do you think that's true? That men secretly hate women?

ASH: I think it's the opposite. Only I don't think it's a secret.

He turns off the TV and throws himself down next to AISHA again. He grabs her book—

AISHA: *ASH!*   **ASH:** *The Female Eunuch?!*

AISHA: A woman who castrates herself in service of her femininity.

She finds a page and hands it back to him.

Don't judge—*read.* From here.

ASH: "This woman paints her face and dreams of white weddings and arranges the home that will be her dreary, sexless prison . . . "

ASH looks at AISHA, who laughs.

For the rest of her *life*?! That's depressing.

AISHA: "White weddings" are depressing!

ASH: Good thing ours was red, then.

She lies back on the couch with her book and sees something stuck inside the back cover. A postcard.

AISHA: Shit.

She hands it to ASH.

This came for you.

ASH: Lake Louise?

He flips it over to see who it's from.

From Samir.

Beat.

AISHA: I stuck it in here so I wouldn't forget and I . . . What does it say?

ASH: You know what it says.

Beat.

AISHA: *(defensive)* I don't know why he doesn't call like a normal person!

ASH: He hates the phone.

(points out a word) **What kind of storm?**

AISHA: *Mountain* **storm.**

ASH: His writing's shit! You read it.

AISHA: *(reads)* "This mountain storm—no monsoon we've ever experienced comes close to it, Ash. The water against the rocks was loud like thunder, yet there were pockets of air so calm ... barely a ripple on the lake. But look up, the vapours swirling above the peaks remind you the battle between the sun and the clouds rages on. When it's over, all that's left is a covering of new snow and a sky like you've never seen anywhere in the world. You would love it, Ash. You guys should come."

ASH: Do you want to go?

AISHA: He doesn't want me there.

ASH *points out the words.*

ASH: "You GUYS **should come."**

AISHA *laughs.*

AISHA: In every photo of the three of us at our wedding Samir looks mad that *I'm* in it!

Beat.

ASH opens a small wooden box.

Now?

ASH: Why not?

AISHA: It's the most fertile day of my cycle.

He lights up a fresh joint. AISHA takes this in.

ASH: I heard Nuzha singing through the wall yesterday. She's been very happy the last few weeks.

AISHA: She's on that bus almost every day.

ASH: Where does she go?

AISHA: She's learning the city—

ASH laughs.

ASH: She could be up to anything! The girl we met that first night could be the complete opposite of who she really is.

AISHA: Okay—you're high . . .

ASH: Sita's friend—Shushma? How many times has that idiot said she was a dancer back home? To *Sita* of all people!

(laying it on thick) **"Do you know, Sita . . . I was a very famous dancer in my city—JUST LIKE YOU!"**

AISHA laughs.

Nuzha can be whoever she wants to be here. She could even invent her *personality* if she wanted to. Who would know the truth? No wonder she's singing through the walls.

Beat.

AISHA: Do you wish you could be someone different than you are?

Beat.

ASH: No.

AISHA: I do.

ASH: You do?

AISHA: If I walked into a bank with a bagful of cash, I still couldn't buy a house or a car unless you—*or my father*—signed for it. Without you to define me, I don't exist.

ASH: Far from it!

AISHA: At home. But out there . . . it's just one roadblock after another.

ASH jumps up and heads for the bedroom.

ASH: I've got something for you!

AISHA: *(flirty)* In there . . . ?

ASH: *(off stage, in English)* **"Don't believe what your eyes are telling you. All they show is limitation. Look with your understanding."**

AISHA: What's that from?

He emerges with a book.

ASH: *Jonathan Livingston Seagull!*

(*excited*) He's pushing the limits of everything he knows about flying. Every day he learns more. If we're willing to push against our boundaries—*or roadblocks*—and open ourselves up beyond what we perceive, then anything's possible!

He flips through the book.

There's a part I want to find for you.

He sits beside her. AISHA *looks over his shoulder.*

AISHA: (*amused*) You're *underlining* . . . ?

ASH: **"Learn nothing, and the next world is the same as this one, all the same limitations and lead weights to overcome."** If we don't *risk* anything, we're just doomed to repeat ourselves!

Beat.

Will you read it?

AISHA: Sure.

ASH: I really want you to.

AISHA: Okay.

He knows she's lying.

AISHA *laughs.*

It's about a *bird*, Ash!

ASH: NO. It's about *freedom*.

Pause.

AISHA stands.

AISHA: Coming?

ASH: In a minute.

She goes to the bedroom.

ASH picks up the postcard, reading it over again. Then, taking one last drag . . . he joins her.

SCENE FIVE

Stairwell. Friday, December 25, 1970.

QASIM enters the apartment building from outside and goes up the stairs. SITA, coat over sari, is on her way out. He sees her first.

QASIM: Where are you going? It's one o'clock in the morning.

SITA: The river. I can't sleep.

QASIM: It's too dark—

SITA clicks her flashlight on and shines it at him.

How was the Christmas party? Sorry I / couldn't—

SITA: Nuzha didn't ask to come here.

QASIM: No one forced her.

SITA: But you did promise to be her husband.

QASIM sits heavily on the stairs, head in hands.

Don't do that—I won't feel sorry for you! If this marriage fails, it will fall on Nuzha's head, *not* yours—

QASIM: I won't abandon her!

SITA: Abandonment is not the problem! If anyone back home finds out that you two . . . *haven't* . . .

QASIM: *(shocked)* She told you?

Beat.

I won't sleep with her out of duty!

SITA: And I suppose you think that's noble?

Beat.

I have a cousin who was impotent on his wedding night and every night after. His bride was desperate. She went to any woman who could help her—for a trick or a potion to make him . . . but nothing worked. He was impotent but they made it her shame. She drowned herself.

He looks at SITA.

QASIM: I love Abby.

SITA: A love is keeping you stuck in the past, my brother. It's time to look to the future.

As she makes her way out:

QASIM: How can someone who holds onto her own grief so fiercely—to the exclusion of all other love—dare lecture ME about the future.

He stands.

You're as stuck back there as I am. But at least I'm not a hypocrite.

SITA is stricken by his words.

SCENE SIX

SITA and SACHIN's place. Later the same night.

SITA enters the apartment, careful not to awaken SACHIN, who is on the bed, arm over his eyes. She steps out of her boots, and as she removes her coat:

SACHIN: You went to the river.

Caught, she doesn't respond. She enters the bedroom. Her petticoat, blouse, and sari from the Christmas party left strewn on the floor.

Gathering them, she begins to fold, her back to him.

SITA: When can you take me shopping? I have a lot of cooking to do before next Friday.

SACHIN: What's happening Friday?

SITA: Our New Year's party.

SACHIN: We just got home from Christmas!

SITA: At the *International Centre.* This one is just for us at home.

SACHIN: Cancel it.

SITA: But you love parties.

SACHIN: I'm not in the mood—

SITA: But I planned everything already.

SACHIN: So change the plan. Is that possible for you, Sita? *To change a plan.*

> *Beat.*

SITA: Are you angry with me?

SACHIN: Just fed up saying yes to you all the time. You're just not used to "no."

> *Pause.*

I was just lying here thinking about the first time I saw you.

> *Through the following, SITA gathers and pleats the sari.*

SITA: At the Rotary Club.

SACHIN: Not at the Rotary Club.

SITA: *Yes*—the fundraiser Amitav organized.

SACHIN: Why do you think I went to that idiot's fundraiser? I wanted to see you again.

SITA: (*confused*) Again?

SACHIN: I didn't actually *see* you at first—not properly. You were turning so fast I couldn't see your face—

SITA: I was dancing?

SACHIN: Dancing *Kali.*

Beat.

Raging at how unworthy we mortals were of this world we'd been given. When Shiva lay down in your path to stop you from killing and you stepped on him by mistake . . .

He sticks his tongue out, like Kali.

You looked so horrified at what you'd done. So *vulnerable.* You stole my heart.

Pause.

SITA: Why didn't you tell me this before now?

SACHIN: I don't know. My own little secret maybe.

SITA: Your own little secret about me.

She sits beside him, sari in hand.

A lifetime ago.

Pause.

SACHIN laughs.

SACHIN: That tin-can airplane you all took to Kashmir!

SITA: No.

Beat.

(*reluctant*) It was Ladakh first.

SACHIN: Right . . .

SITA: We performed for the queen of Ladakh. She gave us a standing ovation.

SACHIN: Gave *you* a standing ovation.

Beat.

And from there on to China?

SITA nods.

SITA: It felt like the whole world was waiting just for me.

Pause.

SACHIN: How long since you let me near you?

Beat.

SITA: I try. I try, but I *can't* . . .

SACHIN: Lose another one.

Pause.

SITA: I miss her.

Beat.

Even *not* breathing in my arms . . . I miss her.

SACHIN: I know. I do too.

Beat.

SITA: It's *different*.

SACHIN: How? She was my baby too.

SITA: I know. I know / she was—

SACHIN: Then what are you saying?

SITA: I *carried* her. It changes you.

> SACHIN *gets up and heads out of the bedroom.*

Where are you going?

SACHIN: I have to turn off the lights.

SITA: What did I say?

SACHIN: You don't have to say it.

SITA: We're finally talking

SACHIN: What does it matter what I say to you?! Your suffering will always be greater than mine.

SITA: That is NOT what I said . . .

(*following him out*) Please.

> *Carefully, she closes the distance between them. When she's near:*

Please.

> *Tentatively* SITA *places her hands on his chest, but the shock of her touch after so long forces him to step back.*

SACHIN: *No, Sita.*

> *Beat.*

What did you say to me? I make you lose everything that matters to you. What do you lose if we do this?

SITA reaches for him again.

SITA: Nothing!

SACHIN steps back again.

SACHIN: You *should go* back to the life you wanted. One without me, one without Leela . . . maybe it's good she's dead—

She shoves him violently.

SITA: *NOOOO!*

Beat.

NO.

Beat.

SACHIN: (*soft*) Go home, Sita. Go home.

SCENE SEVEN

*QASIM and NUZHA's place. Morning. Thursday, December
31, 1970.*

*NUZHA reads near the lamp. QASIM enters from the bedroom
wearing a* kurta *shirt and pyjama pants.*

NUZHA: *(surprised)* You go to the clinic on Saturdays.

QASIM: I told them I was busy.

NUZHA goes back to her book.

Pause. QASIM doesn't know what to do with himself. Finally:

What is that you're reading?

She holds it up.

Kanthapura.

Beat.

The best novel to come out of India according to E.M. Forster.

NUZHA: You've read it?

QASIM: A favourite copy is in the trunk under my bed.

NUZHA goes back to her book.

QASIM tries to busy himself with something. He tries again:

How are you finding it?

NUZHA: *(eyes on the page)* People will fanatically enforce *centuries* of caste discrimination but the moment Gandhi cries "India unite!" suddenly generations of unnecessary suffering is erased—

QASIM: Isn't that a good thing?

NUZHA: Yes, but the hypocrisy is depressing.

Beat.

QASIM: I find it hopeful.

She looks up at him.

NUZHA: How is that hopeful?

QASIM: Deep down I think people want to reach for something better than themselves.

NUZHA resumes reading.

Pause.

My mother marched with him, you know.

NUZHA: Marched with *Gandhi*?

QASIM: When the British made it illegal to make salt from our own sea water, my mother joined his Salt March—a two-hundred-and-forty-mile walk to the Arabian sea. All the women from the village followed her. Even to jail.

NUZHA: Jail?!

Beat.

What happened to them there?

QASIM: Most were let go. They beat and starved my mother though—because she refused to renounce Gandhi. They finally gave up and freed her. They weren't prepared for how stubborn a "simple" village woman could be!

Beat.

NUZHA goes back to her book. She turns a page. QASIM, careful, sits at the far end of the couch.

It's incredible, isn't it? Hindu and Muslim families living peacefully for centuries . . . then fighting side by side for independence, only to lose everything they held precious when they got it—

NUZHA turns another page.

NUZHA: All because of a random line.

QASIM: There was nothing *random* about the Radcliffe Line! Drawing it down the middle of our country was Britain's final "go to hell." They were happy to leave us to kill each other on their way out.

Pause.

NUZHA: Do you think my grandmother was one of those women who followed your mother to the sea? They were friends.

QASIM: You should ask her.

NUZHA: She won't talk about that time. She watched her village burn from a hiding place. That's all I know.

She goes back to her book.

QASIM: I know why it had to be you now. You and me.

She looks up at him.

Any children *we* have, they get some part of their burned-down
village back.

> *NUZHA takes this in—when SACHIN barges in, a box of Lucky
> Strike cigarettes in hand. Seeing QASIM:*

SACHIN: **Oh! So sorry!**

QASIM: **Since when do you apologize for barging in?**

> *SACHIN glances at NUZHA, who immediately heads for the
> kitchen.*

(*to SACHIN, re: carton*) **Those for me?**

SACHIN: **Yes! Uh . . . *yes*.**

> *He quickly hands the enormous carton to QASIM, who laughs.*

QASIM: **Trying to kill me?**

> *At the sink, heart racing, NUZHA pours herself some water.*

NUZHA: **Can I offer you something?**

SACHIN: **I can't stay, / unfortunately—**

QASIM: **Wait just a minute.**

> *QASIM goes into the bedroom. SACHIN heads straight for
> NUZHA.*

SACHIN: **Meet me at my car! I'll wait for you—**

> *She backs up.*

NUZHA: **What are you doing—he's right here!**

SACHIN moves in too close.

SACHIN: I need to BE WITH YOU—

NUZHA, desperate, opens the fridge.

NUZHA: Are you crazy?!

He slams it shut.

SACHIN: When can I see you, then?

NUZHA heads for the sink again.

NUZHA: I don't know!

SACHIN chases her there.

SACHIN: I need to / see you—

NUZHA: I have to go out now!

SACHIN: Where?! *Where are you always going?!*

He stops short as QASIM emerges with a box of expensive chocolates.

QASIM: Happy early New Year. For tomorrow's dessert.

SACHIN: Thanks.

Pause.

NUZHA: We'll see you tomorrow night. At the party.

He goes. NUZHA downs her water, unable to move from the sink. QASIM picks up NUZHA's book.

QASIM: Have you heard of Virginia Woolf?

Beat.

NUZHA: No.

QASIM approaches NUZHA at the sink.

QASIM: She was a contemporary of Forster—a brilliant writer. When asked what use is reading, she said: **"Are there not some pursuits that we practise because they are good in themselves, and some pleasures that are final? And is not this among them?"**

Beat.

We could go to the bookstore and buy you one of her books if you like . . .

He touches her face. Startled, she pulls back abruptly.

Beat.

You have an eyelash. On your cheek.

He gently removes it.

Beat.

Then, suddenly, NUZHA barrels towards the bedroom.

NUZHA: I was trying my sari blouses the other day, the ones Mummy made for winter here, but the arms were too tight . . .

QASIM: That extra layer will keep you warm!

NUZHA searches her night table.

NUZHA: Sita told me about a woman you introduced her to—she brings Sita spices from India . . . *Lochana*—

QASIM: Lochana Arora! We give her a list and she brings it all back in her suitcase . . . charging us double of course!

NUZHA reappears in the doorway, an address book in her hands.

NUZHA: She sews sari blouses in her spare time. Sita couldn't find her number but said you would have it. I looked in your address book for her name.

She opens it to the "L" page.

Lochana.

(*in English*) L, O . . . and I see . . .

She gives the book to QASIM, the page open. He looks and goes pale.

QASIM: Lover.

Directly to QASIM's face:

NUZHA: I remembered Sita's *puja*. How Abby was so sad. How strange you were.

Beat.

I looked under "A" for Abby. It's the same number.

QASIM: I didn't know she did this—

NUZHA: All this time . . . thinking what's wrong with *me*.

She leaves, slamming the door behind her.

QASIM: *(to himself)* I want to be better.

SCENE EIGHT

SACHIN and SITA's place. Night. Friday, January 1, 1971.

SITA's party is in full swing. AISHA dances with ASH to the Bollywood hit "Dum Maro Dum." QASIM pours himself a martini in the kitchen. NUZHA rolls a joint on the coffee table. SACHIN paces, watching. AISHA knocks the reel to reel tape player.

SACHIN: HEY! My brother just mailed me that tape!

ASH: *(to AISHA)* Let's sit for a while . . .

AISHA: I don't want to sit. I want to *dance*—

ASH: Then stop knocking shit over!

SACHIN: *(to NUZHA)* That's too much.

NUZHA: Ash told me to fill it!

SACHIN: It's not supposed to look like a *cigar*—

AISHA: Don't listen to him—it's never too much weed!

SITA: *(off stage)* Can someone turn off the lights?

SACHIN: What the hell is she doing in there?

SACHIN switches off the lights.

SITA: Are they off?

EVERYONE: YES! / They're off! / Come out now!

SITA emerges from the bedroom, her face alight from the flames of diya *lamps reflected on a round mirrored tray.*

AISHA: Oh, Sita . . .   QASIM: Wow.

NUZHA: It looks like Diwali!

SACHIN retreats into the kitchen with ASH's *box to make space for her.*

SITA: And since Diwali marks *our* New Year, I thought why not do the same tonight?

ASH: Diwali for New Year's! Brilliant.

SITA places the tray on the coffee table, then sits in front of it.

SITA: You see the way the light reflects off the mirror? Maybe we could reflect on ourselves . . . for the new year—?

QASIM: A New Year's resolution!

AISHA: Let's do it!

SITA: *(directed at SACHIN)* Can we all come around?

On his way to the couch, QASIM sees SACHIN pour himself a drink.

QASIM: *(surprised)* You're having a drink?

SACHIN ignores him.

ASH: Let me change the music. Something not so "druggy."

AISHA: (*to SITA*) So . . . what do we do?

SITA: I don't really have a plan.

AISHA: SITA JUST SAID SHE DOESN'T *HAVE A PLAN*.

ASH: (*teases SITA*) Do you have a fever?

Everyone but SACHIN laughs.

AISHA: I'll go first! This year I wish to . . . finish my master's.

ASH: You could have done a doctorate in all the time it's taken!

AISHA: SO SICK OF IT!

QASIM: And for the future?

AISHA: My doctorate.

ASH: GOD HELP ME!!!

Everyone laughs again. Indian classical flute music begins to play.

SACHIN: (*to ASH*) That record skips.

SITA: (*to SACHIN*) And what about you? What do you want for the year ahead?

Beat.

SACHIN: To move.

ASH: What do you mean, *move*?

SITA: (*stunned*) You never told me this—

AISHA: You can't move! *We're* here!

SACHIN: Not from *here*. From the International Centre.

AISHA: You scared the hell out of me!

SACHIN: We need our own building. Like the Ukrainians.

ASH: Why? Everyone gets along great. The Filipinos just hosted an amazing Christmas. And when Germany moves into a bigger room next month, we'll get theirs—

QASIM: And rent is a dollar a year, so why move?

SACHIN: *This* is the problem! If we had ANY ambition to share our culture on a broader scale, we'd be contributing to our collective identity as Canadians, not just as an ethnic "side note"—

AISHA: You sound like you're running for office.

QASIM: (*to SACHIN*) When you say broader, you really mean bigger—

SACHIN: I mean more than just a room in a building!

   Pause.

NUZHA: It's not just a room, though. It's all of us together in one place. If one by one every country moves out of that building, we'll be separate again . . .

   SITA confirms NUZHA's sentiment with a touch.

SITA: Like when we got here!

   NUZHA, immediately feeling guilty, discreetly pulls away.

SACHIN: Why are you all so negative? It could be a big step for us—

QASIM: Because even if India *does* get our own building, it's only a matter of time before there's division inside. The Sikhs will want a gurdwara, the South Indians will start to itch for a temple of their own, and you can bet the *Hindu* Bengalis will divide off from us *Muslim* Bengalis—

AISHA: Not necessarily—look at us!

QASIM: It happened back home.

SACHIN: This isn't *Partition*—it's real estate!

QASIM: What do you think Partition was about?

Beat.

SITA: I'll go.

SITA slides the mirrored tray closer to her face.

Sometimes, I get stuck on an idea of how these things—Brother's Day, Diwali, even tonight—how they should go. That if we don't do our rituals right, there's no point doing them. But maybe that's the problem—this idea that there *is* a "*right*" way. If we have the desire to do them—when we're so far from home—how could what we do ever be wrong?

SITA glances at SACHIN—this is for him.

ASH: (*jokes*) I really think she has a fever.

They laugh.

NUZHA: Can I . . . be next?

NUZHA stares into the flames, building up the courage to speak. Through the following, NUZHA keeps her eyes on the lights, not daring to look at either QASIM or SACHIN.

I got a job.

SACHIN: WHAT?!

AISHA: WHERE?!

QASIM puts down his glass. NUZHA clocks this.

NUZHA: Art Gallery.

Beat.

There's a lady there—she explains a lot of the art to me . . . She didn't care I was shy with my English. / She talked to me—

ASH: But how did you get a JOB?!

NUZHA: *(peeks at ASH)* She's the manager of the cafeteria there. When one of their staff quit before a school tour, they were short . . . I said I could try to help—

ASH: *(incredulous)* Just like that?

NUZHA: *(timid)* At first she said, "You don't look like you need a job," because of . . . how I look—

QASIM: You *don't* need a job.

NUZHA: *(still to ASH)* But I really liked it.

SACHIN: You told me you were exploring the city.

NUZHA: How much exploring can one person do?

SITA: How long has this been going on?

NUZHA: Two weeks. **Part-time.**

Taken aback, SITA looks at QASIM for a reaction. He has none.

ASH: (*delighted*) **"Part-time"**—listen to her!

AISHA: What's the job?

NUZHA hesitates.

NUZHA: (*into the candles*) I was mopping at first but / then—

SACHIN: Mopping the *floor*?

NUZHA: —because the mop was too heavy for me to lift when it was wet, I started breading chicken.

SITA: You're *cooking*?

NUZHA: It's easy when they show you how.

ASH: She's amazing. Isn't she amazing!?

NUZHA: (*shy, to ASH*) At lunchtime it's hard because you have to keep pace with the person doing the frying. Especially when the schools come because chicken fingers are their favourite—

AISHA: (*impressed*) I don't believe this . . .

NUZHA: I wanted to tell *you* right away, Aisha, because I knew you would be happy, but then I was scared I might get fired because I was so slow—

SACHIN: Why didn't you tell me this?

SITA: Why would she tell you?

AISHA: And you really like it there?

NUZHA: Oh, I love it! Every day I walk in, somebody always says, **"Glad to see you, Nuzha! Hi, how are you today?"**

SACHIN: They don't mean it—it's just what people say.

ASH: And that's an asshole thing to say!

NUZHA: (*directly to* SACHIN) They do mean it. They're my *friends*.

> *Taken aback by* NUZHA, *SACHIN heads to the bar.* SITA *takes them in.*

You all have something.

> SITA *gets up.*

(*to* SITA) Like your dancing—even if you don't do it here, it's still yours. Now I have something of my own too. And I'm good at it.

SACHIN: (*scoffs*) Good at breading chicken!

NUZHA: (*pushes back*) **Number one best "breader" for December!**

> *Pause.*

QASIM: Good for you.

> *Everyone is surprised.* NUZHA *looks at him for the first time.*

NUZHA: You mean . . . I can keep working?

QASIM: Sounds like they would be lost without you.

NUZHA, relieved, beams.

My turn.

He stands.

I know I've put you all—my dearest friends—in an impossible situation these last few months. So, first thing—I want to acknowledge how unfair that was. But, more importantly, I want to address my behaviour . . .

(*to NUZHA*) With you. This coming year . . . I'd like to step back from the practice and spend more time at home. I'm hoping this might be a . . . humble start to the reparations I need to make. For the way I've behaved since the day you arrived. If you're willing.

NUZHA is speechless.

Through the following, no voices are raised.

SACHIN: (*pouring a drink*) How is "working less" a reparation for being an ass?

QASIM: By acknowledging that I've *been* an ass.

SACHIN: So . . . a kind of awakening?

QASIM: You could call it that.

ASH: (*to SACHIN*) What he's saying is good! Why are *you* being an ass?

SACHIN: Did I say it wasn't good? I'm just saying that it's more of the same from him. All about what Qasim wants WHEN HE wants it—

QASIM: That's the opposite of what I'm saying, / actually—

SACHIN: As if the people his actions have affected have no say in the matter—

QASIM: She *has* say! None of this works if Nuzha isn't agreeable—

SACHIN: (*turns on* NUZHA) Are you, Nuzha? Are you . . . "agreeable"?

QASIM: (*confused*) **What is up with you, man?**

SACHIN: **She's mopping the fucking floor, man.**

ASH: Cool it, Sach—   QASIM: (*to* SITA) If he goes on like
                                        this, we have to go.

SACHIN: Please go. Because *we* can't stand watching you think you can undo the hell you've put her through because of a sudden flash of conscience—

AISHA: Hey, don't speak for me!   QASIM: I *know* what I've put her
                                        through.

SACHIN: (*speaking over* QASIM) Because you don't get to decide the consequences after months of being a cold, narcissistic *son of a bitch.*

NUZHA stands. SITA reacts.

QASIM: Okay, we need to go.

As QASIM *takes* NUZHA's *hand,* SACHIN *grabs her opposite arm, pulling her to him.*

SACHIN: DON'T YOU TELL HER WHAT TO DO.

Everyone freezes. A stunned silence.

(*to* NUZHA) Ask him the last time he slept with Abby in your bed.

(*to* QASIM) *Tell* her.

QASIM *won't.*

Two *days* before you got here.

NUZHA *walks out.*

You coming here ruined everything for him!

After a moment QASIM *follows.*

Pause.

AISHA: Let's go.

ASH: (*to* SITA) Do you want us to?

SITA *doesn't—can't—respond.*

Sita. Do you want us to stay?

AISHA: NOW, ASH.

They go. SACHIN *doesn't move.* SITA *doesn't move. Finally,* SITA *picks up the tray, and blows out the lamps, one by one . . .*

The record skips.

SCENE NINE

ASH and AISHA's place. Moments later.

AISHA kicks off her shoes. ASH throws himself on the couch.

ASH: Holy *shit.*

AISHA: Maybe he's just in love with her.

ASH: No. They're fucking.

AISHA: He wouldn't take advantage of her like that.

ASH: Why do you assume *he's* the one taking advantage?

AISHA heads to the kitchen.

AISHA: It's my fault.

ASH: Why? Did you lend them our apartment?

AISHA: I told her women should lead independent lives!

ASH: And she listened! You should feel proud.

AISHA: Breading chicken is hardly a giant step forward for feminism.

ASH watches AISHA pour herself more wine.

ASH: Why don't you have some tea?

AISHA: *(sharp)* Why? Do you want some?

AISHA brings her wine over and snuggles up against him.

ASH: It's something, though, isn't it? That girl who arrived dreaming of marriage and babies didn't crumple . . . she just / changed course—

AISHA: Slept with Sita's husband.

ASH: Took charge of her life.

Pause.

l need to wash this night off.

He disappears into the bathroom. The shower comes on.

AISHA hums the tune to "Dum Maro Dum." Downing her wine, she gets up and grooves a bit—her sari slips off her shoulder . . .

An idea.

Taking the end of her sari, she ties it to the bedroom doorknob, giggling as she does. The shower turns off. ASH emerges, only a towel around his waist.

AISHA begins to unwind herself from her sari . . . slowly, sensually, singing the lyrics to "Dum Maro Dum" as her sari unravels across the length of the living room to where ASH is standing.

AISHA reaches her arms around his neck, ready for a kiss, when ASH moves her arms gently off his neck and looks into her eyes, not letting go of her hands.

Aisha.

AISHA starts kissing him. He pulls his face away.

You need to . . . I need you to . . . *know* something—

She grabs his face, desperate.

AISHA: Tell me one thing I don't know about you—*TELL ME ONE THING I DON'T KNOW ABOUT YOU, ASH*—

Her legs collapse, but he won't let go. They sink to the floor.

You don't want me.

ASH: I love you.

AISHA: But you don't *want* me—

ASH: I like . . . men. But I *love* you—

AISHA: Don't lie to me!

ASH: That was never a lie, Aisha! *Never.*

AISHA: But *children* were!

She falls against him, sobbing. He encircles her with his arms.

Pause.

ASH: (*with great tenderness*) What if we can take what makes us . . . *different* . . . and build something beautiful?

Beat.

Any child we have will have two parents who see each other, Aisha . . . really *see* each other. What greater love than that?

He holds her tighter.

Beat.

(*whisper*) We'll find our own way to be happy.

SCENE TEN

SACHIN and SITA's place. Midnight.

SACHIN: Sita?

(*louder*) Sita. Are you in the bathroom?

SACHIN emerges from the bedroom, disoriented and hungover. He checks the bathroom, then goes to the window to see if she's gone to the river.

Turning, he sees the flashlight. She's left it behind. He panics. Rushing for his coat, he trips over his boots. The door opens.

It's SITA: resplendent in a red parka, cheeks red from the cold.

(*collapsing with relief*) I thought—

Beat. Beat.

Where did you go?

SITA: I walked.

Beat.

There was a crowd—I got scared—a little girl . . . she took my hand, pulled me to the front—

SACHIN: The front of—

SITA: The *line*. For the last trolley ride that will ever happen here. We were the lucky ones. That's what the little girl said.

SACHIN: (*in disbelief*) You . . . got on?

SITA: So many people waiting to get on! Even when there was no more room, they were at every stop, waving—taking pictures! We sat at the back . . . an old lady passed a flask around—and it was so good what it was—like apples but hot. Children singing . . . and the little girl who would *not* let go of my hand. When we got to the bridge, there was the biggest crowd of all—so many flashbulbs! A man was crying—like for him it was the end of something. When we passed the doughnut shop, I got down . . . I know the way back from there.

She pulls out a slip of paper.

The little girl's mother gave me this.

She hands it to SACHIN.

SACHIN: Vera Smith.

SITA: *(taking it back)* If I call, I only have to say my address and she'll pick me up. The little girl wants me to see her do ballet.

Pause.

SACHIN: Are you leaving me?

Beat.

SITA: I felt . . . something with those people. Those strangers. I wasn't there missing Leela, or there but afraid without you. When we passed the river, I saw huge pieces of ice rushing by so fast and I thought, maybe she moved like that—our baby. Maybe she floated fast from that dirty shore, into the middle, then into the ocean, and then another and another until finally . . . she came here. To my river.

Beat.

Do you think so? Do you think . . . she could be here? With us?

SACHIN: Could you believe that?

Beat.

SITA: I want to try.

SCENE ELEVEN

QASIM's bedroom. Midnight.

In bed, NUZHA is still in her sari, but QASIM is in pyjama pants and an undershirt. They lie on top of the bedspread, their backs to each other.

NUZHA: In all these months, this is the first time we've been on this bed together awake.

Beat.

You don't want to ask me anything?

QASIM: What should I ask that I don't already know.

Beat.

What do you want?

NUZHA: I don't know. No one ever asked me that before.

Beat.

What if I told you I want to study at the university—like Aisha? Or the school where they teach you to cook? My friend at the cafeteria goes there.

Beat.

QASIM: I would say we should look at each of those things together.

NUZHA: What if I told you I alone want to choose what happens next. Like you did—

QASIM: I didn't *choose* anything!

NUZHA sits up immediately.

NUZHA: You wanted to be a doctor—you're a doctor! You wanted to come to Canada—and here you are! The only thing you didn't choose was me.

Pause.

NUZHA summons courage, her eyes fixed ahead.

You promised I could decide my wedding dowry when I was ready. That whatever I wanted, you would give it to me.

QASIM: Yes.

NUZHA: I want a divorce.

Beat.

He sits up then, speechless, and stares at her back, but she doesn't dare look at him. QASIM walks out of the bedroom. NUZHA remains on the bed, unsure what to do next.

QASIM: (*from the living room*) And what's your plan? Do you even have a plan?!

NUZHA: I don't want to go back / home—

QASIM: That's what you *don't* want! What I'm asking is WHAT DO YOU WANT?! Run off and get married—

NUZHA: NO!	QASIM: (*continuous*) —I'll take care of Sita. Sachin doesn't have to worry about her—

NUZHA: *I DON'T WANT SACHIN. I WANT MY LIFE.*

Beat.

QASIM *sits heavily on the couch.* NUZHA *remains on the bed.*

Say something.

QASIM: You want a divorce. What is there to say?

Pause.

In Quranic law, if the wife initiates . . . a divorce . . . she's required to give something in exchange for her freedom. The suggestion is that she forgo the right to her dowry.

NUZHA: They mean money. I don't want your money—

QASIM: But if the *husband* initiates the divorce, he can choose to honour the terms of the dowry.

Beat.

NUZHA: I don't know what that means.

QASIM: It makes better sense I should divorce you.

Beat.

He comes back to the bedroom doorway.

What if I told you I don't want to?

NUZHA: You don't love me.

QASIM: I care about you.

NUZHA: But you don't *love* me!

QASIM: I don't know how to do this!

He leaves again. Overcome, he tries to steady himself. When he's ready, he speaks the words out loud, but not to her.

Our families can't know. Not yet.

NUZHA: Because of your mother?

QASIM: Because no matter what reason I give for this divorce, they will never look at you the same way again. I won't ruin your life.

Finally, he comes back into the room and sits on the end of the bed, eyes fixed ahead. Through the following, QASIM, strug-gling, does not look at NUZHA.

The divorce can't be your dowry. Your entitlement to a dowry is a term of the divorce.

NUZHA: How do you know all this?

QASIM: I looked it up the day we got married.

She laughs, surprised.

What do you want to study?

NUZHA: I don't know.

QASIM: What do you love to do?

NUZHA: I don't know.

Beat.

How can I go to university if I don't know?

QASIM: That's what university is for. To discover what you love.

NUZHA: I'd . . . like to do that.

Beat.

QASIM: Then the time and the money to discover what you love shall be your dowry.

Pause.

NUZHA: What love will you discover?

QASIM shrugs.

Abby?

QASIM: Life doesn't work that way.

NUZHA: But it could.

Beat.

NUZHA gets off the bed and sits down next to him.

Beat.

QASIM: Shall we . . . ?

Pause.

What do we do?

NUZHA: I don't know.

They can't help but laugh.

QASIM: "I divorce thee" three times?

NUZHA: I think so.

QASIM: It seems so cold.

Beat.

NUZHA: Then do it . . . as a blessing.

She takes his right hand and places it on the top of her head, her own hand remaining over his.

We can be people of our own making now . . .

QASIM: *(tenderly) Talaaq.*

NUZHA: Me, because of you . . .

QASIM: *Talaaq.*

NUZHA: And you . . . because of me.

QASIM: *Talaaq.*

She takes her hand off of his. He gently removes his own. They look at each other as if for the first time.

End of play.

Pamela Mala Sinha is an award-winning Canadian actress and writer, working internationally in theatre, television, and film. Pamela is the recipient of Canada's prestigious Dora Mavor Moore Award for Outstanding New Play and Outstanding Lead Actress for her solo debut play, CRASH. Published by Scirocco Drama, CRASH was also included in Bloomsbury UK's *Audition Speeches* anthology and in *Love, Loss, and Longing* (Playwrights Canada Press). Her second play, *Happy Place*, premiered in Toronto at Soulpepper, followed by runs at Vancouver's Touchstone Theatre and Winnipeg's Prairie Theatre Exchange. CRASH debuted in the US at the Signature Theatre, NY, as part of Soulpepper's tour in 2016. As one of few artists selected nationally to receive a prestigious Project Imagination commission from Soulpepper, Pamela began research for *New*, which she completed as playwright-in-residence at Necessary Angel Theatre Company. Pamela's film adaptation of *Happy Place* was produced by Jennifer Kawaja (Sienna Films/Sphere Media) and directed by Helen Shaver. Pamela completed development with the CBC and Sienna Films on her series *Nirvana* and production wrapped in 2022 on the film version of CRASH (produced by Necessary Angel and Riddle Films) starring Pamela. Pamela is partner to playwright and mathematician John Mighton and proud stepmother to Chloe.